"Since I last saw you I have put a number of things into action. I now feel I'm on the way to making music my full time career rather than just a hobby"

Lois Paton
International composer
www.skylarkmusic.org

"Ryan finds a way to reach a deeper level in his workshops and make his audience realize that they already have the necessary skills and talent to showcase their creative expression. It was a truly insightful and eye opening seminar"

Marcus Powell
CEO of the Crescendo Trust of Aotearoa
www.ctoa.co.nz

"Ryan's wisdom is second to none. I highly recommend Ryan Kershaw's coaching to my students and peers alike, as I want them to experience his motivational energy so he can aid them as much as he has aided me"

Danny Champion
Live audio engineer.
Founder of DC Sound

"I have attended several of workshops and mentoring/coaching sessions held by Ryan. After the first workshop, I have already gained an insight and perspective into the NZ music industry and above all seeing myself in it. Since then I have been able to set clear goals and targets, from writing a biography, to planning and preparing pre-production for my first album. I have met key individuals, local to the music industry, that are able to provide valuable advice and experience when it comes to recording and having material played on the radio

Simon Randle
Wolfshield Guitar Tuition, United Kingdom
www.simon-randle.wix.com/wolfshieldtuition

"I went to see Ryan Kershaw in the planning stages of my album release. I followed his advice, which lead me on a path of learning and invaluable connections."

James Castady-Kristament (JCK)
Hip Hop Artist and Music Reviewer

"I came to Ryan looking for a teacher who would improve my playing and specifically work on genres that interested me. Needless to say it was obvious from the very first lesson that Ryan had an extensive grasp of these specific topics but also a wealth of knowledge about the guitar and its techniques, a wide range of different musical genres and the music industry. What sets Ryan apart from other teachers is not only his outstanding technical ability but also the fact that he has been around the scene and done it all"

Carl McWilliams
lead guitarist of Oslo Brown.

"Ryan is more than a highly accomplished guitar player. He is, importantly, a listener: not just of music of all types (of which he is very knowledgeable) but he also listens carefully to his students. Consequently, Ryan does not teach you to play the GUITAR, he teaches YOU to play the guitar."

Eric Taylor
Guitarist and Webmaster for the Guitar Association of New Zealand

"My son Samuel first started guitar lessons with Ryan when he was 7 years old. Sam immediately liked Ryan. His friendly way, and his ability to relate to a younger student in an engaging way was evident from his first lesson.
His tutoring is second to none. Ryan is a wonderful mentor and the techniques Sam has learnt from Ryan has set him up for life. I asked Sam this morning – "How would you describe Ryan?" "Mum, Ryan is cool and he rocks."

Sara-Jane Morgan

"After six years of being a frustrated guitarist, I decided to take lessons because I just couldn't make the guitar sound even bearable. Tried everything from learning simple covers, to jamming with drums, other guitarists, YouTube... the list goes on. With Ryan we decided it was time to unlearn a few things and get back to basics, go over concepts I already 'knew'. "David Gilmour can take you to heaven and back on just four notes" said Ryan. He continued, "that's the art you need to master and in no time you'd be climbing up and down the neck". After 6 to 8 weeks, strictly on only a four notes of the pentatonic, I was jamming to every goddamn thing, even gansta pop! Stevie Ray Vaughan, The Sex Pistols and Bo Diddley were my new idols. I have been taking lessons for 9 months now and the growth is just exponential. I never knew it would just take 9 months of lessons with Ryan to pick up the guitar and sound like I know what I'm doing, more importantly, feel great that I can confidently pick up a guitar, with riffs and improvisation."

Tapan Mujerki

Workshop feedback from the Bachelor class of the S.A.E Institute
- *"I feel like I can grow my career and personal traits with the inspiration you've given me"*
- *"The group activities were excellent, inspirational guy"*
- *His people skills were great, learnt so much and he kept people engaged through the entire day.*
- *Fantastic guy, will be seeing him again. 11/10!*
- *I thought it was simply going to be a step-by-step guide on becoming an established muso, but I found it incredibly inspiring.*
- *Expectations met, above and beyond!*
- *I loved how Ryan created an evironment where all of us as aspiring music professionals felt uninhibited and free to be honest about our careers*
- *What did you enjoy most about this lecture? Hearing about Ryan's background and how he became successful in his business*

USE YOUR BUZZ TO PLAY THE GUITAR

RYAN KERSHAW

Cover by Ryan Kershaw and Aaron Palatchie
www.aaronpalatchie.com

Layout by Polgarus Studio
www.polgarusstudio.com

National library of New Zealand cataloguing-
In-Publication Data
Kershaw, Ryan, 1983-
Use your buzz to play the guitar / by Ryan Kershaw
ISBN 978-0-473-25318-9
1. Guitar – Instruction and study
2. Guitar – Methods 1. Title
787.87076 – dc23

Dedicated to guitarists all over the world who are working hard but feel stuck. That feeling doesn't last, as long as you keep learning.

Contents

Acknowledgements

Thanks to these special people who made the process of getting this book completed a lot easier

Sarah Thomas, Raia King, Deb Englander, Martha Bullen, Ann McIndoo, Steve Harrison, Geoffrey Berwind, the team at Bradley Communications Corp, my Quantum Leap journeymen and women

And especially my Dad

The doors of the theatre were closed but I could hear the crowds outside.

I was facing the projector screen at the back of the stage, watching the psychedelic spirals and images work their magic as the smoke rose and filled the room with an enchanting haze. The doors unlocked and hundreds of kids ran inside the theatre. This was it. This is what I had planned and seen in my mind. This was my time. I looked over at my drummer. He counted in 'one... two... three... four...' I turned around and there was a sea of smiling faces as the music kicked in. For that brief moment they had forgotten the world. They were not worried about the past or the future; they were just where they needed to be.

And so was I...

- Ryan Kershaw recalling his high school concert with Paradox at 16 years of age

INTRODUCTION

WHY I WROTE THIS BOOK

When I was starting out, I didn't get any help from people in the music industry. My parents weren't rich and I had no 'connections in the business.' I faced many obstacles.

This is the book that I wished someone had given me.

There are hundreds if not thousands of books on learning the guitar, but *none* have focused on the best **ways to think** as you are learning. None have focused on creativity and finding **your own sound**. With music in mainstream media not terribly appealing these days, I strongly believe that we need to re-discover our creativity. My hope is that by using this book, you will not only learn a lot more, but you will also subconsciously 'learn how to learn better.'

Using this book should be just the start of your guitar playing and you should use it in conjunction with other books and learning material. However, even this introduction will help guide you to a lifetime of enjoying music at a higher level.

HOW TO USE THIS BOOK

This book alone will not make you a great guitarist. It is up to **you** to do that. No one else can do that for you. This book is, however, one of the best tools available to help you learn how to play guitar at a high level.

Read this book thoroughly more than once. There are subtle things that you may miss on the first reading that you will pick up on the second or third.

Use the *Use Your Buzz to Play The Guitar* workbooks and ***do the exercises provided.*** As I always say: When you know something, that is good. When you understand something, that is better. When you understand and **apply** knowledge in a positive practical way, that is when you will get the most out of life.

Share this book with your friends and family because playing music with other people is one of the best things you can do as a musician.

To get the most out of this book, use the *'Use Your Buzz…'* **notebooks** alongside the workbooks, then you will be well on your way to making astounding improvements on the guitar no matter what level of experience you currently have.

Also listen to the *'Use Your Buzz to Play The Guitar'* **audiobook** everyday to condition yourself to think like a professional and achieve the best results possible.

Chapter 1 - How to Learn: Redefine 'Study'

"The greatest gift I received from being a teacher was the increased ability to continue to learn" - Ryan Kershaw

Everyone Studies Whether They Realize it or Not

I used to have a strong dislike for the word study. I didn't study in the traditional sense at school and you may switch off as soon as you hear that word too. You may think that you don't study, but the truth is that everybody studies something. Studying doesn't mean sitting down and cramming your head full of facts and figures at the last minute for a test. Study can be defined as the devotion of time and attention to acquiring knowledge. I'll say that again—studying can be defined as the devotion of time and attention to acquiring knowledge, and everyone acquires knowledge on something throughout the course of their lives. For some it might be through experience on how to be the top dog in jail; others may acquire knowledge of street drugs through experience. But they have still studied, through watching people that they hang out with and asking questions.

Like me, if you don't like studying in the traditional sense, it might pay to redefine study and realize that by seeing study as a positive thing that you continuously do, you can learn and progress towards where you want to be much quicker. You have studied those who have influenced you and imitation is a big part of how people learn. When you are an infant, you copy the actions of your caregivers; you imitate the sounds you hear with speech, you copy expressions to convey how you feel. In the same way, a great deal can be learned from imitating technique, or even subconsciously copying how your favorite performer moves on stage, which brings me to my next point:

Learn From Different People

Three great role models are better than one and are certainly better than one dodgy role model. Learning from different people helps you a lot because you are getting the knowledge from different sources. It also helps you develop a signature style. It's tempting to want to copy your favorite guitarist but , but if you just copy them, you are going to end up as a clone. You won't have your own signature style, which is really where most people want to go to with the guitar. They want to be able to express themselves personally. And that's the cool thing about guitar; it's such a personal thing. Learning an instrument is the greatest expression of your soul. Once you can master an instrument enough to be able to communicate what you're feeling with other people, it is amazing. Learning from different guitarists will enable you to mold these different influences into your personal style of playing.

Learn From Different Places

As well as learning from different people, you can learn from various places. There are so many resources now— the Internet, organizations, libraries, local tutors, your friends etc.

Some people learn visually while others lean more towards auditory or kinesthetic ways of learning. In other words, some people like to watch and then they learn best by watching someone else. Other people like to listen to a recording which lets the information sink in more easily. Find out which way you like to learn the best. I recommend you try and learn every way. Just because you're better at learning visually doesn't mean you should cut out listening to things or vice-versa. So try and learn from different methods.

One thing with learning that is really important is to learn the why, and not just the what. Most people learn what something is, but they don't know *why* something is. Learning why gives you a better understanding of what you are doing. For example, why is an A major called an A major? Or, why would you want to do a hammer on? Why would you want to do a hammer on instead of just picking? Why is a certain guitarist respected the world over? Learning the why also gives you the ability to select the right tools to express the sound that you have in your head or your heart when you play. Learn the why, not just the what.

Your Practice Conscience ™

The last thing I want to talk about in this section on how to learn and redefining study, is practice. Many of my students ask how I practice and how much should any student practice? Well. every guitarist has what I like to call a practice conscience. Some teachers will say half an hour while other teachers will say an hour. I personally think that I probably don't even need to tell you. Your practice conscience will tell you if you've practiced enough or not. You know if you've had a good practicing session. If you haven't put any effort in throughout the week on something that your teacher has shown you or something that you're trying to learn, you know that. You don't need to tell anyone else and you're not fooling anyone else either. When you have your next lesson and you haven't practiced, your teacher is going to know that. He or she can see it straight away. So listen to your own practice conscience.

Still, I think that half an hour every day is a good minimum and concentrated practice for half an hour a day is better than eight hours of unproductive practice. What I mean is that if you practice really well for half an hour, that's more productive than if you spent hours practicing, but interrupted by phone calls, watching television or really not putting much effort into your practice. You probably have heard the phrase time management; really there's no such thing as time management because time can't be managed, but you can manage yourself. Read about what is commonly called 'time management' if you need some tips on managing your busy schedule; or you can divide your practice up in the same way that you divide up a constructive day. If you write down at the start of your day five things that you need to do or feel you need to do, and you actually go out and do those things, you're going to feel more productive at the end of the day. The same principle can be applied to practice.

One last thought on practice: Nothing new can come from practice without *creativity*...

Exercise 1.1 Developing Good Habits

It is so important that you start this course with good habits. It is small 'bad', or 'unhealthy' habits that can be the cause of much struggle in life. Think about it – when someone is overweight, it has not happened with one big feast. Generally that person is overweight because of poor habits, the results of which have accumulated over time.

The same principle works in regards with learning an instrument. Small habits over time make the majority of the difference. You need discipline to practice regularly and effective time management habits will help to lessen the feeling of being overwhelmed or 'snowed under'.

Begin by getting two notebooks. Label the first **'What I Learned'** and label the second notebook **'A Bit Each Day'**.

You will use the 'What I Learned' notebook to write down ideas taken from songs and exercises, and can even note down ideas as you watch music documentaries or live/recorded performances.

The 'A Bit Each Day' notebook is for you to write down what you do each day with this course, and with your practice. It is a small but helpful habit, as if you don't have the discipline to write one or two sentences in a notebook each day, how will you develop the discipline to get great at playing the guitar?

Get the two notebooks now and start the habit of using them today.

Exercise 1.2 Gaining Focus of What You Like

Picking your favourite guitarist might seem like an overly simple exercise – but it is highly beneficial to be aware of who you respect musically.

Having a guitarist that you admire means that you can have something to aspire to and it also provides a bit of inspiration for your learning.

Even for advanced players, this can be quite important as there are many challenges one can face as an amateur or professional muso, and thinking of who inspired you early on can remind you of what impacted you as a music fan and made you want to play.

Write down who your favourite guitar player is and if you are not sure, this will be a great opportunity to do a bit of research on guitar players. Often with solo artists the singer will be known, but the guitarists name might not be as well known, so if you have a favourite singer you could look into who their guitarist is.

My favourite guitarist is _____

Exercise 1.3 Expanding Your Knowledge

Expanding your awareness and appreciation for musicians that you havent heard of before not only helps to expand your knowledge, but can also boost your playing skills too.

In sports, learning from one role model is good but after a while there is a danger of becoming a clone of that person. If you learn from various role models you can take ideas from each and eventually form your own style.

It is exactly the same with learning guitar – there are many great guitarists so don't limit yourself by learning from only one.

For this exercise, find three guitarists that you have not heard of. It might pay to find who influenced your favourite guitarists, or use a site such as Wikipedia to find guitarists related in some professional way to the guitarist you listed in exercise 1.2.

Guitarist 1 _____

Guitarist 2 _____

Guitarist 3 _____

Exercise 1.4 Learn How To Find Help!

My method of teaching in '*Use Your Buzz*' will help you to help yourself learn more effectively. If I just gave you the name of a website to help you learn the guitar, it would not be as beneficial to you as getting you to make lists, and find new ways of learning that you can apply to other areas of life and continue to use for years to come.

When you are needing to get information, it is wise to think of various formats and places that can help you. It is easy to feel overwhelmed so breaking it down into categories can help.

List some resources in the table provided below, or make your own version with pen and paper or on a computer document. Remember you can use this whether you are wanting to learn a new sport, find help with recording, learn more about the industry etc.

For now – lets focus on where you could find help with learning to play the guitar:

Websites/Online	(example = www.ryan-kershaw.com)
People I Know	(example = your friend who plays in a band)
Libraries	(example = list local libraries in your area)
Local Teachers	(example = local guitar teachers)
Other	(example = workshops, retail outlets etc)

Exercise 1.5 This Can Help When It's Tough!

Knowing WHY you want to play is a life-saver in times of self-doubt. We all go through periods of not feeling great about our guitar playing, even those of us who teach guitar!

Remembering why you want to play can keep you on track towards your goals.

For this exercise write down why you want to play, and what you would eventually like to do or get out of being good at the guitar. You may want to be a rock star, or you might just want to be able to strum a few chords at home to relax...

I want to play because

_____

_____

_____

_____

I want to improve because eventually I'd like to

_____

_____

_____

• Use my *Guitar Goals* poster to help you. Download the poster and print to A2 size (you can download it to your usb/flash drive and take it to a stationery shop where they can print it for you). Get it laminated with a gloss finish and then you can use a whiteboard marker to write down your goals and tasks.

Exercise 1.6 Your Practice Conscience™

From now, devote a minimum of half an hour every day to practice.

It can help to structure your practice and start by memorizing theory, then warm up with the chromatic spider exercise or easy song. If you are practicing chords, focus on getting one or two strum patterns sounding great, rather than lots of chords but no rhythm to them.

Memorise the song that you are trying to learn by getting chunks of the song at a time, and turn over the page of the music when you are trying to memorize it – to see if you can play it without looking.

If you are learning how to improvise, leave that for later in the practice session and take the time to really experiment with your techniques.

I recommend finishing with something easy or enjoyable, and remember that half an hour of solid practice, uninterrupted and without distraction, is better than an hour of mucking around.

Listen to your Practice Conscience this week. Practice for at least 30 minutes every day and stick to good habits with practice.

It will pay off!

How Using This Chapter Will Help You

Everything starts with the mind. Regardless of how well you can play technically, if you don't have a positive attitude towards improving, you are missing out on so much. This chapter addresses the often overlooked core of learning, which is the way that you think, and is the start to making big jumps forward on your instrument.

This chapter will help you start to
think like a professional guitarist

Chapter 2 - Creativity and Experimentation: How to Find Your Sound

Find the Benefit in Every Song

There's a great quote by Napoleon Hill in which he says: "For every failure there is a seed of an equivalent or greater benefit," and the same can be said for the songs that you learn.

I know what it like to go to a teacher and receive songs that you don't like. But if this is happening to you or you're trying to learn something that you're finding hard and its putting you off, try and find out what the benefit is that is hidden inside what you are doing.

For example, if you're trying a new song and you have recently started learning what hammer-ons are or what pull-offs are, it might not be a great song but it might be helpful to put the work in that's necessary to improve your technique.

The benefit of this is that once you practice that song enough, other songs with that same technique will seem easy. At least the part of doing that technique will seem easy.

There's something that you can learn from every song if you're open to it. If you come in thinking, "Well, I'm not going to like this song," or "I don't know this artist,"then your learning will be slowed down by these excuses. But if you try and find something in every song that will help you and you realise that you can progress by putting the work in, then you will learn more quickly.

Turning negatives into positive plays a big part in getting through rough times in life. There will also be times in your playing when you don't feel like you're a good player or nothing's happening with your band, or your parents say that you have to give up the guitar. Perhaps your husband is giving you grief because you're spending too much time practicing. You need to learn to turn negatives into positives in order for you to get through life without being stressed by everything.

Find the benefit in what you're doing and remember the benefit of what you're doing. Try and find a new chord or a new technique in the songs that you're learning. It might spark off an idea for a riff. It might give you an idea for an original song.

A big one is to read about the artist of the songs you're playing, especially if you don't know who the artist is. You don't know all of the best artists in the world. Think about your favorite musician. Did you always know who they were or were there times when you hadn't even heard of them?

Right. So, if you thought you already knew everything about music, you wouldn't have discovered them and they wouldn't have changed your life. Keep that open attitude towards musical discovery. No matter how many bands you know, there are a million more just as good that you haven't discovered yet.

Not all of the greatest bands in the world are on mainstream music channels or on T.V. Go to a shop, dig out some albums and listen to some music that you haven't heard before. There's so much music waiting to be discovered.

Try Out New Techniques

Experimenting with a new technique is a great way, as mentioned earlier, to spark off a riff or an idea for a song. Changing the techniques used in a riff can change it for the better.

Why do you play a hammer-on? You learned it and someone showed you it, but why do you do it? It is designed to make the run or the pattern of notes sound smoother. Try it, try three notes in a row on the same string - 1, 2, 3. If you pick each note, notice how it sounds. Jagged like a staircase.

Now, try the same notes again but pick only the first note and hammer the second two. Does it sound smoother? It should if you use the technique correctly.

Changing the techniques in a song can change it for the better. If you do a slow slide, you may notice that you get the bumps of the frets in between. So if you're getting that annoying sound try hitting the first note that you hit, but instead of a sliding up to the note - 2 frets above, try bending so that the pitch raises to a sound that is the same as two frets above.

A bend will give you a smoother sound than a slow slide of the fingertip across the fret wires. Techniques can even become signature aspects of a guitarist's style. Think of Zakk Wylde who was most famous for playing guitar for Ozzy Osbourne but also has a number of great projects on his own. Check out Black Label Society if you're not already familiar with his sound.

He has a very distinct style and I would definitely say his signature technique is the *pinch harmonic,* that high pitch squeal that you can hear in many of his songs. Or Chuck Berry and his *double stops.* Chuck pioneered a way of playing with double stops that continues to this day.

Just a side note: If I talk about a term such as double stop that you don't understand, take a minute to look up the meaning of the term. That how you learn. If someone's talking to you and you don't know what a word means, ask the person what it means.

Zooming In On Techniques

One thing that I do quite often and I think is great practice is to zoom in on a technique. What I mean by that is, if you're a rock player and you do *pick slides,* how good are you at controlling the exact sound you have with those pick slides? Chances are you just do it randomly, maybe a slide down into a chord.

But did you know that you can actually control that sound by focusing say half an hour a day, even just one day, focusing for half an hour on the pick slide itself. Try it. If you slide slow with the pick, scrape it along the string slowly; it creates a different tone than if you use the side of your hand fast. Try scraping along the D string and then the E string; see if there's any difference.

Knowing these things allows you to slowly develop control of the technique you're using. This applies to any other technique, not just pick slides.

There's a video I have on YouTube which imitates dolphins and whale sonar. A friend of mine who runs a tattoo studio asked me to make a sound similar to that of dolphins. In the video, I used the pick slides to create a sound similar to that of the dolphin and whale sonar. Having the ability to know those subtle differences gave me control of what I was doing.

Tune the Guitar Differently

Unlike a piano, guitar strings can be easily and quickly tuned to different notes. The standard E tuning that most guitars come with, whether you've bought the instrument in a store or from someone, is that the low thick string is E, the next string is A, and then it goes D, G, B, and E again.

But you don't have to keep the strings to these notes. You can use the tuning pegs on the end of the guitar to tune them to any letters that you want to. You might tune the guitar G, D, C, A, E, B. It might not sound great but that's the cool thing, you can make up these different tunings. You can get some really interesting sounds by just changing one string. That is common, especially with drop D tuning.

You can also use the tuning pegs in songs. I've made a track called *Tribal*, that resembles a tribal feel. In the track one can hear a diving, descending bass sound of a guitar note. The way I did that was with a string winder. I tuned the string low first and then as the drums were hitting in the background, on beat 4 I'd strike the string and quickly wind the string loose with the string winder, and it created a descending diving sound.

A really great example of how to use the tuning pegs in a song, is *passionflower* by Jon Gomm. He is an absolutely brilliant guitarist and I suggest you look up his video online. My dream is that one day the majority of music on mainstream media and television will be of this quality – though with big business the way it is, it is unlikely.

Something else that you can look into is *open tunings*. Open tunings are when you tune the guitar's strings to the notes of a chord. For example, a C chord is a combination of the notes C, E, and G. If you tune you're guitar strings to become these notes together, it means that when you strum the strings with no fingers on the strings it will be a C chord.

So for example, if you take your first finger and barre the second fret in this tuning, two frets up or a tone up; this will become a D chord. Open tuning is a very common tuning for slide guitar because the slide fits flat in a direct line across the strings.

Some other examples of tunings include Nashville tuning where you actually change the thickness of the strings and *slack key tuning*. Try and see if you can find some other examples.

Here are some guitarists who have used open tunings:

Ani DiFranco
Billy Corgan
Keith Richards
Ryan Kershaw
Jimmy Page
Bob Dylan
Duane Allman
Jack White
Elmore James
David Crosby

Poly Chords, Cluster Chords and Your Chords

Poly chords are multiple chords put together. These often get confused with slash chords. Slash chords are the chords where you see two letters separated by a diagonal line or slash. What this means is that you should play, for example, a C chord with a G bass note.

This would be represented by C/G. The left letter represents a chord; the right letter represents a bass note, just a single note. Poly chords are when you have two whole chords together. For example, if you play a D major chord in its open position, usually the first D major chord that you learn. Play a D and then add an E5 power chord on top of that.

Going down the strings from the thick string, you would have the thick string open. The next string would be on fret 2, the next strings note would be on fret 2, the string after that would be on fret 2 also. The second to last string would be on fret 3 and the very thin string, again, would be on fret 2. This would be a D chord mixed in with an E5, so played together, this would be called a $\frac{D}{E5}$. That is a poly chord.

Another example of a different style of chord that you might like to try are *cluster chords*. Cluster chords are not technical so if you went over to a piano and just smashed your hand on any random keys, that could be considered a cluster chord. Technically, that would be some type of chord.. You could analyze it and find its correct term. But for the sense of pure creativity, just slam your hand down on the piano and see what it comes up with. You can use that; you can use anything you want to make sound.

In the Fleetwood Mac song, *Second Hand News*, the musicians use tapping on a chair. You can use anything as long as it gets you the right sound. Although there are benefits for knowing, you don't have to know the technical terms for what you're playing in order to sound good.

How about your chords? Have you got a chord that you would like to play or one that's your signature sound? The 7#9 chord is commonly referred to as the Hendrix Chord. Could you use the poly chord idea or the cluster chord idea to find a signature chord that you could use?

The Creative Guitarist

"Instead of competing all we have to do is create" - Earl Nightingale.

If you want to become creative, know that you are already whether you realize it or not. You can see how creative you are by following the lead of guitarists who have already established a reputation as being creative themselves.

A list of creative guitarists who you might like to check out include Frank Zappa, Chet Atkins, Michael Hedges, Dick Dale, and Partyzant.

Frank Zappa is universally respected by musicians around the world for being one of the few musicians you could say is truly unique. He had multiple influences from classical to contemporary and wasn't afraid to show his individual character in his songs. He approached it in a contemporary pop format but more like a composer; he used the different instruments of a rock band almost like an orchestra.

A young guitarist named Steve Vai was Frank Zappa's protégé and I would suggest checking out his playing since he has become one of the best in the world.

Chet Atkins pioneered a way of playing that sounded to the listener as if there were two guitars, but there was only one. He would play a bassline with his thumb and then use his fingers to come up with the melody for the song. This style of playing has influenced many guitarists including one of my personal favorites, Tommy Emmanuel.

Michael Hedges took that way of thinking and expanded on that. If you haven't heard *Aerial Boundaries,* I suggest you look it up now; take any acoustic percussive way of playing which thanks to the Internet has been exposed in recent years and you can hear his influence. He is really telling a story with just the sounds of his guitar.

Dick Dale almost single handedly started the surf guitar movement and his use of tremolo picking developed his signature sound.

Partyzant is a great guitarist who can be found on online. (It's an example of how modern technology can expose guitarists to an audience that might not have otherwise seen them.) He approaches the guitar almost the same way as a piano; and really the guitar is just a piano without keys but we'll save that for another book.

Pick the Lock with a Different Combination

After a while your fingers get used to going in the same combinations on the guitar. Try it; pick up your guitar and see what you play - it's probably quite familiar.

What you might want to do is sit down and try starting with your second finger if you always play something with your first, or if you start with your third, try starting with the second. Create a riff from there that sounds a little different from your other riffs.

Another idea to get your fingers working in different ways is to write on a different instrument. Because you play the guitar already, or some of you will, you will be used to playing it in a familiar way. Try playing on an instrument such as a piano that you're not used to. Because you don't have any technique on the piano, you will have to think in a purely creative sense and you will come up with a different combination than what you'd usually play on the guitar. Try coming up with something on the piano and then put it over to the guitar and see what it sounds like. Then you might want to play that riff backwards, slow it down, speed it up, try the notes in a different order etc.

Pick the lock with a different combination.

Of course, learning theory can give you more tools to be creative with. It will also open you up to musical rules that you can have fun trying to break.

Exercise 2.1 How To Learn More Effectively

You can get much more out of playing songs than just playing the song itself.

Some of the things to discover and learn from include: New techniques and ways of applying them, structure ideas (how the songwriter orders the sections of the song), use of dynamics (loud and quiet / volume changes), guitar effects, amp settings, scales and chords etc.

For this exercise take a song that you are currently learning and look deeper into the song to extract ideas from it. Study the things mentioned above and how they are put into the song.

If you are not currently learning a song, pick a basic song to try this with. You can even get ideas from nursery rhymes such as 'Twinkle Twinkle Little Star' (the repetition of the 3rd phrase, the 'rhyming' of the melody, the picking technique or position of the notes on the fretboard).

Write your observations down in your **What I Learned** notebook alongside the days date. Get into the habit now of using songs to your advantage by looking deeper at what is going on.

Song: _____

Artist: _____

Observations:

_____

_____

_____

_____

_____

_____

_____

_____

_____

_____

Exercise 2.2 Getting Your Own Style

Take a chord, technique or idea from the song that you picked in exercise 2.1.

Experiment with it as much as you can and turn it into something different. If it is a chord you might pick various combinations of strings and play using a *broken chord* idea, or if it is a hammer-on you could make it a trill and use it for your own lick.

(Remember if you don't know what a word such as lick means in reference to playing the guitar, use a dictionary or online search to find the definition).

Write down the chord, technique or idea in the space provided below and also write how you changed it. Again – it is wise to note down these observations in your **What I Learned** notebook, as well as the spaces provided on these pages.

Chord/technique/idea:

_____

How I Changed It:

_____
_____
_____
_____
_____

Exercise 2.3 Express Your Creativity

As human beings we are naturally creative.
For some it might be building, for others – Art. For a lot of us though, it is music!

It's time to start getting creative with your guitar playing. You don't need to be a professional to make things up; as long as you keep it basic you can end up with something that's pretty good. If you try and make something too complicated, it is unlikely that it will sound good to begin with, so to start – keep it simple.

A riff is a short repetitive phrase played with single notes or chords. The main parts of the famous classic rock songs Smoke On The Water, Sweet Child O' Mine, and Iron Man are all riffs. Riffs can be found in all styles of music – from Rap to Reggae, Classical to Jazz.

Make up your own riff and use Tablature or notation to write out your riff. If you don't know how to write Tablature (commonly called TAB), find an instructional video online to help you, and then write down your idea on the lines below. The letters to the left represent each string name, with the upper case 'E' representing the thickest string at the bottom of the page.

e _____
B _____
G _____
D _____
A _____
E _____

Exercise 2.4 Always Tune First

Having your guitar in tune is a necessity. If your guitar strings are out of tune, you can hit the right notes but they will sound like wrong notes (provided of course that sounding in tune is an aim).

The first thing to do here is to get a tuner that works well and has new batteries. It is useful to get a **chromatic** tuner, and make sure that it is able to pick up the sound of acoustic guitars as well as electric. Some tuners also come with an in-built or digital **metronome**.

The second thing to do is to watch a video on tuning your guitar by ear. If you are playing a live show you should always use an electronic tuner to check your tuning, but tuning by ear is an important skill to have so you can quickly tune if you are jamming with friends or are somewhere without a tuner.

Search "guitar tuning ear lesson" and find a video that you can easily follow, though keep in mind that it does take a bit of time and practice to get good at tuning by ear.

This is a practice which should not be avoided, so make sure that you do not skip this step.

Write the Url/internet address of the video below:

Tuning video:

_____

Exercise 2.5 Learn From Good Examples

It is nice to take a break from physical practice and study, by watching an inspiring performance from a performer who is skilled at the craft of playing the guitar.

In the previous exercise we talked about tuning the guitar. This exercise is to listen to examples of how guitarists actually use the tuning pegs creatively in music.

For the first example, you can listen to my track 'Tribal', a short piece of music that I made for a friends tattoo website. I called it 'Tribal' as it has that kind of a feel and you can hear me using the tuning pegs to create a descending sound.

I loosened the string first so that it was already a little slack and low sounding. Then on just the right beat I picked the string and wound fast with a string-winder to create that diving sound.

For the second example search online for a video called 'Passionflower' by Jon Gomm. It is a brilliant example of what one can do with just the voice and an acoustic guitar!

Success leaves clues. Learn from good examples.

Exercise 2.6 Don't Be Too Rigid

Not everything has to be overly technical when it comes to music and it pays to break up the focused study and research with a bit of fun.

For this exercise - make up your own chord. Put your fingers on different combinations of notes that you have not played before, until you get a chord that sounds great, and give that chord a name.

Once you have done that, use my Notes Of The Fretboard poster to try and figure out which notes (letters) you are playing, and find out what the chord is actually called.

It's a bit of fun and gets you thinking outside of the box. You will also benefit from getting creative and making a riff using this newly discovered chord.

<u>How The Content in This Chapter Will Help You</u>

Every human being is creative, although as we get older a lot of the spark gets knocked out of us by other people's negative opinions or what we perceive as unsuccessful attempts or failures. Unlocking your creativity will bring you more joy on the instrument and allow you to discover even more ways to express yourself.

Using this chapter will help you to become creative.

Chapter 3 - Why Theory Helps: Learn More Tools to Break More Rules

Knowing more is never a bad thing if it is used in a positive way. Many people are afraid of theory and it's really a shame. I empathize because people are afraid of what they don't understand. When I started I didn't like theory and I'm not saying I'm that much of a guitar geek that I spent eight hours a day reading only theory, talk only about theory to my friends, and can't wait to the weekend so I can buy a new theory book. Though, at the same time I know that it is important and it can be used creatively. Usually the guitarists who don't understand theory come up with the old argument that theory makes you sound technical and that is absolute nonsense..

Theory does not make you sound too technical; using theory only makes you sound too technical or void of feeling if you approach it in that way. Hitting notes that you don't want to hit isn't usually a good feel when you're really getting into a riff or solo, so do not be afraid to utilize theory as another tool for when you need it.

Notes of the Guitar

I'll say it now and I want you to remember this— *the notes of the guitar are the most important things that you will learn to understand music theory.*

I know what it feels like to not want to learn them but it is worth it. It opens up everything else that you will learn in terms of music theory—how chords are made, why you play scales, where you play them, just about the whole thing.

There are various ways of learning the notes on the strings. You can find so many methods on the Internet that you can look them up yourself and I don't need to go over them in this book. The same applies to the C chord. I don't need to show you how to play a C chord. There are already thousands of books that show you how to play C chords.

One of the ways of learning notes that is often recommended is to learn them in blocks or positions and while useful for notation, I think my preferred method is to learn the notes along the thick string first. Learn them along one string because then on the other strings, they're actually in the same order, just at a different starting point for each string. Also, learning them along the thick string gives you a starting point for a lot of scales.

Take your time to learn the notes. If it takes you six weeks to learn one string, then that is fine; learn that string and then go into the next string. Don't try and rush and learn all the strings in one week. That will just scramble your brain.

Power Chords

Power chords are a very common and versatile shape in music. They're not strictly major or minor so it sounds good over both. In other words, when you're playing a song, if you play an A minor instead of an A major it'll probably sound pretty terrible. But if you don't know whether something is major or minor, chances are the power chord will work.

You can find out more about how to do a power chord shape in my *Use Your Buzz* online course, but I want to explain the construction of them so you understand again how theory can actually help you.

If I told you to learn say 20 different names and what they are, and you haven't done that before, that would probably take you a while. How long does it usually take you to learn 20 chords? It would take you a few weeks at least. Well I'll tell you in two minutes how to do that.

The most common type of power chord is called a 5th and there are different types of power chords; you can classify 3^{rds} as power chords as well but for now we'll focus on the 5th.

A 5th is actually a type of interval; it's not technically a chord. A chord is when you have three different letters put together, so for example a C, E and G is a C chord. Now I could have 20,000 C's being played and 20,000 G's, how many notes is that? Forty thousand? No. It's actually two; two distinct notes but a lot of each one. Twenty thousand of the note C and 20,000 of the note G; but two different notes: C and G.

So a 5th or power chord is technically an interval. An interval is a gap of a certain amount. If you're a doctor and you're monitoring a heart beat and you see on the heart machine the little rise in the line representing a heartbeat, and then a gap then another *heartbeat*, and there's a gap of a second, that gap is called an interval of a second. In music, if you have a gap between notes of a certain distance, that gap is called an interval.

If you have the notes A and E being played that's called an A5 because it starts at A, and if you count from A to E - A, B, C, D, E, that is five, so it is called an A5.

Now using that method on the thick string, play a power chord at the 5th fret. The 5th fret is an A so this would make this power chord an A5. Remember, it's a 5th because the first finger and the third finger are placed on notes that are five apart, A and E.

Shift the power chord to the 3rd fret. It's now starting at the note G on the thick string. This makes it a G5. If you move this up one fret to the 4th fret, this becomes a G sharp 5. You can also call a G sharp 5 an A flat 5.

Now this might be a lot to take in for if you have not done notes or power chords before, but I suggest you use the book and do a bit of research yourself and this will make perfect sense. Be aware, that knowing theory, knowing the notes of the strings allows you to unlock all of these chords straight away, instead of taking weeks, months or even years to learn them all.

Pentatonics

The same thing can be applied for pentatonic scales.

A pentatonic scale is a 5-note scale and probably the most common scale in contemporary music. Although I suggest that you learn the major scale first if you can, since everything else is built from the major scale including the pentatonic, we'll focus on the pentatonic for now.

If you don't know what a pentatonic looks like go on YouTube and look up a lesson. You can do just as much with one well played pentatonic as you can with five half-good scales.

A really great example of this is the second solo in the song *Comfortably Numb* by David Gilmour of Pink Floyd. It's an absolutely brilliant solo and one I like to play live, but 99 percent of that solo is just that scale. Look up the tab for *Comfortably Numb* and you will see that the notes for most of the solo are based around the 7th fret pentatonic shape.

It's the little techniques that are going to put your life into that scale. You can learn the remaining shapes of the scale, and you can learn a hundred different scales, but all you're really doing is learning how to put your fingers on different notes. You have to learn what to do with those notes.

As with the power chords you can find where to start by the notes of the thick string, so try this tactic. If you're already somewhat used to the pentatonic scale, try putting on a YouTube backing, type in "smooth backing in A". Open that backing track, let it play and try the pentatonic starting at the 5th fret. The 5th fret on the thick string is an A. This means that it will fit in with the key of the backing track.

Playing scales to backing tracks is a more interesting way to practice and it gives you the feel of playing along to a band.

Tones, Semi-tones and the Major Scale

Tones and semi-tones are the foundation of music in the western world; everything else is based upon these.

Tones and semi-tones are one of those things that when you first learn them, it seems that you can't learn them or you won't use them. Though, as you progress things in music tend to link up like a jigsaw puzzle and you'll use these more and more.

A major scale is what all of the scales in the western music are based from.

Many people learn major scales by learning what a C scale is and spend months memorizing that, and then learn a G scale and spend months memorizing that. I can tell you how to learn a scale in two minutes, which will then allow you how to learn all the major scales at once.

There is an underlying pattern to it. The pattern goes like this: tone, tone, semi-tone, tone, tone, tone, semi-tone. What this means is that if you start at an A note and move up a tone, and then another tone, a semi-tone, three tones, one each, one at a time, and then a last semi-tone, you would have just played the A major scale.

If you do that same pattern but from a C note on the guitar. you will play a C major scale.

This is how you can learn all of these major scales at once. Learn the pattern underneath by learning the theory of the scale.

The good thing about learning the theory of scales is that you can apply it to different instruments like the piano. If you want to make a demo, or if you want to make an album and you want some cool synth backing, or something atmospheric – from Pink Floyd style to Cradle of Filth style - You can apply the same theory to the piano or keyboard as that which you would use on the guitar.

Singing to Scales

On T.V, you may have seen musicians singing along to the piano to practice getting their voice in tune. Well you can sing to scales on a guitar as well.

If you just sing into thin air without anything to lock against, chances are you might be a little off key or off tune. But singing to tuned notes of an instrument gives you something to lock in against and to practice singing in tune to. It can train your voice and it can help you sing well, which is great for when you're at parties. After all, no one wants to sound like a drunk parrot.

How Chords are Made

Another reason a major scale is important is because all the basic chords come from the scale. Once you have the tone, tone, semi-tone, tone, tone, tone, semi-tone pattern down and you understand that, then you can start to find out where all these chords you're playing come from. For example, if you write out the notes of a C scale - tone, tone, semi-tone, tone, tone, tone, semi-tone from C you will come up with the notes C, D, E, F, G, A, B, C.

A major chord just comes from that. A 'C' chord is the 1st, 3rd and 5th note of a C scale put together. A 'D' chord is the 1st, 3rd and 5th note of a D scale put together.

A major scale has the same type of sound, and a major chord has the same type of sound no matter what key; it is just higher or lower.

A minor chord sounds different than a major chord. Knowing and being able to recognize the difference helps you when you're writing songs. It helps you to know what to use to establish the sound you have in your head.

And remember: Don't fall for the trap of believing that you can't understand this. If you are smart enough to invest in yourself by reading this book, then you are smart enough to learn what I am telling you. YOU can do it, even if there aren't people close to you that can help you.

Exercise 3.1 Learn The Strings

* A reminder that each exercise in Use Your Buzz... is able to be adapted to your skill level. For example, if you have already mastered standard tuning, go on to other tunings, or even key frets such as the fifth fret – A, D, G, C, E and A. You can time yourself calling out the letter names of each string as you go down the 5th fret, and get quicker with practice. See the Use Your Buzz To Play The Guitar Intermediate and Advanced/Professional workbooks for more ideas.

Learning the names of each string is helpful in situations where you are talking with other musicians or learning from a friend or teacher. Strings are referred to in numbers and/or letters. For example – the '1st string' is the 'high e string', the second string is the B string etc.

An *open string* refers to playing a string on it's own, without pressing any fingers down. You can use an acronym such as Elephants And Donkeys Grow Big Ears to help you remember the names of each string.

Note: Elephants represents the thick string.

Write the names of the *open strings*:

6th String (thick)   _____
5th String   _____
4th String   _____
3rd String   _____
2nd String   _____
1st String (thin)   _____

Once you have these comfortably memorized and can point out each string if asked randomly, proceed to memorize all of the *natural* notes on the thick string.

Exercise 3.2 Power Chords are 5ths

Power Chords although tricky at first, are very versatile and once you have your fingers around them so to speak, will be a staple part of your guitar playing diet.

An interval is the distance between two notes, and power chords are a type of interval.

For example, if you played the notes A and E, the difference between those two notes is a 5th (A, B, C, D, E = 1, 2, 3, 4, 5) *

So an A note and an E note played together = 'A5'
*Note that in music you count the first note as '1'.

You can have power chords called 3rds and 4ths but generally when someone mentions a power chord, they are meaning what is technically called a '5th'.

For the sake of clarity, write down why a power chord is called a 5th:

_____

_____

_____

_____

_____

_____

_____

Exercise 3.3 The Start To Making Solos

The minor Pentatonic scale is the most common scale used by Rock and Blues players, though it can be found in all styles of playing – and should be something that you aim to master without any excuses.

Watch my video on how to use the 50X Method and in it you will see me play the minor Pentatonic scale as an example. The task for this exercise is to use my 50X Method as the video suggests to memorize this scale.

Do not skip this step – it is an important part of your progress.

Once you have practiced the 50X Method each day for one week, you can then improvise (make stuff up) by changing the order of the notes that you play. It's similar to playing hopscotch with notes – the notes to hit are still located on the same frets, but you can hit them in any order and use combinations.

After changing the note order you can add your own techniques like *slides* and *hammers*. Although I don't encourage skipping exercises on the first run through of this workbook, you may refer to my 'Six Steps to Scales' method to help you master the Pentatonic scale.

Once you get fluent at improvising with the Pentatonic scale, this is where your real expression on the instrument can begin. It takes a bit of practice of course but when comfortable with improvisation you can really start to express your feelings, moods, and creativity by using the instrument.

...

You can also play over most songs that you enjoy using the Pentatonic scales so stick with it!

Exercise 3.4 This Is Important

The Major scale is the most important scale to learn in regards to understanding how music theory works in Western music. It may seem a little intimidating but once you get a good understanding of the Major scale, things like 'how chords are made' (chord construction) make more sense and you will be very glad that you put the effort in to learn it.

Most guitarists will learn one Major scale, say for example 'C Major' and then they will learn another in a few months time… maybe 'G Major'.

**I can save you an enormous amount of time
by giving you a 'secret formula'
(okay it's a known pattern, but secret formula sounds better!)
to memorize all of the Major scales at once!**

Before I give you the formula you will need to understand semi-tones and tones. A *semitone* is the distance of one fret, and a *tone* is the distance of two frets. So for example if you go from an 'A' note on the guitar to an A# (which is up one fret), that means that you have moved up by a semitone.

If you go up two frets, that is going up by a **tone**.

One fret = semitone, two frets = tone

So… the secret formula for memorizing any Major scale can be found in Chapter 3 of *Use Your Buzz To Play The Guitar*.

Re-read this chapter and write the secret formula below:

Pattern for 'Major' scales

To change to a different Major scale simply keep the same pattern, but begin the pattern on a different letter or note.

Exercise 3.5 Memorize The Major Scale

Take a week to memorize the Major scale. Start on the 2nd string (the 'B' string)

For this exercise, your home base note (commonly called the tonic) is on fret 1 of the 2nd string. This is the note that you can come back to if you get lost a bit whilst you are practicing or improvising.

Pick/play that note and then follow the pattern for the Major scale across the string, remembering that tone = two frets and semitone =1 fret.

Doing this will give you the C Major scale, because you played a Major scale starting at a C note (fret 1 of the b string is a C note).

Tip: the name for what I've called a 'home base note' is a 'root note' if used in a chord or 'tonic' if used in a scale. Think of it like the roots of your family tree is where the name of your family comes from. The root note in a chord is where the name of that chord comes from; so a C Major chord comes from a combination of notes in the C Major scale, and the Root note/Tonic is 'C'.

Exercise 3.6 Improvising – Play Over Music

After you've taken a week to really memorize the Major scale inside out, use a C Major backing track to help your improvisation.

A backing track is simply a piece of music, usually with one of the instruments or vocals removed, that you can use to practice your scales and improvise over.

You can find backing tracks for both the Major scales and Pentatonic scales online. Simply type in 'C Major backing' and, if you wish – you can also add a genre such as 'Blues', 'Classical', or 'Metal'.

Use some of the creative ideas from Chapter 2 of *Use Your Buzz To Play The Guitar* and fill in your 'A Bit Each Day' notebook with a record of what you practiced.

Remember that **you should be using the notebooks every day.**

You might like to write down the sites you found or the url's for your preferred backing tracks:

Site/url: _____

Site/url: _____

Site/url: _____

Exercise 3.7 Understanding Chords

It is extremely useful to know how chords are built
(this is called 'chord construction')

It is beneficial simply for the security of knowing and
understanding, but also for a better understanding of why your
fingers have to go where they go for each chord, and for the
increased ability to use chords more effectively – a desirable skill
whether your goal is to play around a campfire or be a virtuoso.

You can also use this knowledge to play chords on other
instruments. A 'C' chord on a piano is comprised of exactly the
same notes as a C chord on the guitar.

Use your copy of *Use Your Buzz to Play The Guitar*, plus any
additional online videos or resources to help you understand
what a Major chord is, and fill in the answers to the questions
below.

How do you make a Major chord? (what notes of the Major
scale do you put together)

_____

_____

_____

Do Major chords generally sound sad or happy?

_____

Do minor chords generally sound sad or happy?

_____

Refresher question: What are the names of each string when tuned to Standard E tuning?

_____

_____

_____

How This Chapter Will Help You

Reading this chapter and applying the knowledge to your playing will help you to change any negative ways of thinking about theory that you might have, and to eliminate your fears of learning more theory!

If you already appreciate theory, using one of the 'Use Your Buzz' workbooks will help you to form a stronger connection between your theory and creativity.

Chapter 4 - If You Can't Afford a Teacher: What to Do If You're Stuck For Help

"When the student is ready the teacher will appear" – adaptation of a line from Light on the Path a book written by Mabel Collins in 1886

One of the first things to do if you're learning the guitar and when I say learning the guitar I mean at any level is to get rid of all your excuses. People often say they can't do something because they can't afford a teacher or they don't have the time, or this or that. These are just excuses. If you can't afford a teacher, that's a concern. But you can still learn on your own and with help from other resources.

There are some easy steps to take to get started. One of the first things you can try is moving chords up and down the guitar. What I mean is that when you learn a C chord, actually when you learn anything, don't just learn it at face value. Try and play it backwards, change the note order and just see what happens.

Take the chords C, D, E, and A Major. If you don't know them, use the Internet or a book to help you. You can play them where they are but you can also shift them up and down the neck. So you know how you play a C chord starting on fret one, or fret three, depending on how you look at it, you could shift that up five frets along the strings. Some places will sound good, some places will sound bad, but you just try it.

Moving chords across the guitar is good for several reasons and for different levels. At a beginner level, it helps you get the co-ordination between both hands without changing shapes. If you find that you've got a strum pattern but you can't change chords very well, moving the same shape across the neck means that you're moving both hands but it's a little simpler than trying to change whole shapes with your fretting hand.

At an intermediate level, it's a great exercise to help master the more difficult rhythm patterns. If you have a strum pattern that you're finding really hard to play, or you're not so good at rhythm, try playing it first without moving the chord. *Don't try and change chords if you haven't got the strum yet;* get the strum while you're holding the chord in one place. Then once you feel comfortable with the strum, rather than changing to another difficult shape, try moving the chord up and down while strumming.

Advanced players can use these basic ideas too. Advanced players might come back to this basic idea to spark off a riff or a motif for a new song. Sometimes, the simplest things are the best.

Learning Songs by Ear

When I started guitar I had a few lessons with a teacher but my teacher didn't teach me the type of music that I was in to. The songs that I learned were by country and western artists but what I really wanted to learn was rock.

I would try and learn what I was shown but at the same time when I was at home I would listen to my favorite Black Sabbath songs and Nirvana albums and try and play songs just by listening to them.

It's a really good exercise to try and teach yourself some things by ear. You may not be teaching yourself but "learning yourself." In other words, your friend might say that he taught himself a Green Day song, or everything he knows on the guitar he taught himself, but was he shown by someone else how to play a C chord? Where did he get that information? He must have gotten it from somewhere? Did he get it off the Internet or from a magazine? Someone has taught them or put the information out there. He has just been open to learning it.

One idea for learning songs by ear is to study *perfect pitch*. Perfect pitch is the ability to recognize a note by hearing it. For more on this, check out articles on the Internet.

Another way to develop your ear is by practicing *aural recognition*. This is just a fancy name for recognizing what's happening by hearing it. Some instructors in music classes at schools are still stuck in the old ways of recognizing intervals by counting the semi-tones. For example, they'll play two notes on a piano, they'll listen to the first note and then try and count the interval between the second. I think this is a primitive method and I think the better method to follow is by recognizing what type of sound something makes. For example, play a 5th on the guitar and now play a flattened 5th; which means that you make a power chord and with the finger that does the 5th of the chord you take it back one fret, you flatten it.

Now notice that this flattened 5th makes almost a horror movie sound. If you play an octave (look it up if you don't know what an octave is) it has a different sound than a flattened 5th. An octave sounds more harmonized for want of a better word, whereas the flattened 5th sounds like something from a horror movie. Listen to what type of sound these different intervals make.

Another benefit of this is that when you're playing your own music or writing your own songs, knowing what type of sounds these intervals make allows you to write your songs more easily.

Guitar Magazines and Fanzines

You may wonder whether it's better to learn from print publications or the Internet. You should take advantage of both sources. Learn from everywhere. There are some great magazines out there such as: Guitarist, Guitar World, Acoustic Guitar, Guitar Player, Total Guitar, Guitar Techniques, and Guitar Aficionado.

A fanzine—a publication originated by fans of bands who decided to make their own magazines and hand them out on the streets. Fanzine = Fan Magazine. They're usually free and tell you where the local gigs are.

Looking at the credits for magazines also opens you up to new career possibilities. Try picking up your local guitar magazine; look in the staff credits/contact section and it will have different types of jobs that people do. While you may not have heard of some of these jobs, they may be a perfect fit. If you're thinking of a career in music, have a look. There are many more opportunities than guitarist, sound engineer and producer. It's your job to seek them out.

Research players in the magazines and books that I have mentioned. Read what they say and you'll get some useful advice.

Internet Teachers

On the Internet, there are countless free videos full of useful advice from respected teachers around the world. You can find the online course to accompany this book at www.ryan-kershaw.com

When you receive helpful knowledge from any of these resources, use repetition to stick to it. That brings us to our next chapter…

Exercise 4.1 Moving Chords

As stated in *Use Your Buzz To Play The Guitar*, moving chords across the fretboard as you play is a helpful exercise for players of all levels. For beginners it increases ones ability to move their hand without their chord shape collapsing, and is useful for focusing on improving rhythm patterns – taking away the extra challenge of hard chord shapes.

At an intermediate level, players can use this approach for mastering more difficult strum patterns. If you have a challenging strum pattern or progression in a song, work on the strum pattern without moving the chord first, then once you do that – change the same shape up and down the fretboard whilst strumming, rather than changing whole shapes. This can result in mastering the rhythm and coordination between both hands quicker than you would if you tried everything straight away.

Advanced players can use these things to spark ideas for a new song, and can add more advanced techniques or chords.

1. Pick a chord that you are most comfortable with. If you have not learnt any chords yet, try the 'A Major' or 'E minor' chords. Once you are used to playing the chord you have chosen, try it in different locations across the fretboard. For example, if you are using 'A Major' you can try it at fret 4 instead of fret 2, and it will give you a different sound (note: that will also change the name of the chord but that is not important at this stage).

If you already know a few chords, try it with C, E, G and A or with a new chord that you are learning.

2. Put a basic rhythm to it and make the chords flow from one place to the next. If it is too difficult just use four downstrokes on fret 2, and then four downstrokes on fret 4.

3. Put in a weeks solid practice with this. After the first week of this (and only after that) start to include and put together other ideas that you have learned such as 'broken chords' and 'arpeggios'.

Exercise 4.2 Learning Songs By Ear

I encourage all of my students to welcome productive advice on playing the guitar from any source that is well informed and credible. Something else that I recommend that you should try and do is to learn your favourite songs by **listening** to them. This is called 'learning songs by ear'. I have put the word 'listening' in bold as a lot of guitar players hear the music, but they don't really listen to it at a deeper level.

As well as feeling a sense of accomplishment, learning songs by listening to them will develop your musical ear. You will start to hear instruments that you didn't hear in the song before (bass guitar is a great example of this). It also gives you insight into how you can layer different instruments when recording to obtain different textures and effects.

Here are 3 approaches you can take to learning by ear:

1. Using Bass Notes and 5ths

Pick any song that sounds as if there are only a few chords repeating over and over. Try and pin point the starting note to the first chord on the thickest string. If it goes 'chord 1, chord 2, chord 3, chord 4' you only try and match 'chord 1' each time with a single note on the thick string. When you have chord 1 matched, then you would try chord 2. And so on until you have all four chords/notes matched. Once you have the whole section done, convert to powerchords (5ths) for a slightly fuller sound.

2. <u>Open Chords</u>

This way is suitable for acoustic songs, or those performed in a singer/songwriter style. Same as above but use chords like A or Am, D Major etc.

3. <u>Using Keys and Scales</u>

If you have a better knowledge of music theory, you might like to figure out which scale fits and work out the chords from there – e.g. If it sounds like it starts on the root note of a C, and a C Major scale fits, then try chords from the Key of C. You can work out scales for solos according to the chords used too.

Take a week to figure out part of a song that you like by ear and record your progress in your What I Learned notebook. Be patient – getting to learn songs by ear takes more than a week, but this will be a good start to acquiring a skill that you can use for the rest of your life.

Exercise 4.3 Guitar Magazines

Guitar magazines are a brilliant resource for your learning.
I personally collected guitar magazines as I was growing up
(and still do), and reading through the articles and interviews
did a lot to both educate and inspire me.

Write the answers to these questions on the lines provided:

1. Is it better to learn from magazines or the internet?
    (*note: it may not be a 'yes or no' answer*)

    _____

    _____

    _____

    _____

2. Where can you look in magazines to find career possibilities?

    _____

    _____

    _____

3. Buy a guitar magazine for this exercise. What magazine
    did you buy?

    _____

    _____

    _____

4. List of places I can get guitar magazines (include local shop names if possible

_____

_____

_____

5. List as many guitar magazine publications as you can think of/discover:
    Ryans tip*: This list can be used later when looking for job opportunities/interviews/publicity and much more*

_____

_____

_____

_____

Exercise 4.4 Use Your Resources!

Often the place where we can find the help we need is looking us right in the face and we don't even see it!

1. Using the guitar magazine that you bought for the last exercise, find two guitar players that you have not heard of before:

    a. _____

    b. _____

2. After reading the magazine, list some things that you learned from it in your 'What I Learned' notebook.

3. To help with your learning and to also support what I do, go to my facebook page and 'like' it. You can find it at www.facebook.com/ryankershawnz

You will find free guitar tips there, as well as advice for personal growth and self development.

If you share some of my videos it not only supports what I do, but more importantly it gives you a mindset of helping others, and not trying to hoard information yourself. Many guitarists and guitar teachers get insecure and try to hold on to information, and are scared to support other musicians and music teachers for fear that they themselves won't do as well. It actually has the opposite effect, and by helping others from a genuine place you will increase the level of respect you get from others. It will also work out much better for you as a musician. Fear nothing, don't become bitter, help others!

Exercise 4.5 Ryan Kershaws 50X Method™

Use my **50x Method** TM at a minimum of twice per day this week to help you memorize something that that you are trying to learn.

My 50 times method TM is an effective way of memorizing sections of music that you can use for licks, solos and riffs. Basically it is repeating the riff 50 times but breaking it down into sets of 10, each with a distinct purpose:

1st set of 10: **Initial Run-through**
This first set of 10 is just to 'suss out' the basics of the riff and get your fingers moving.

2nd set of 10: **Correct Technique**
The second set of 10 is for you to focus on your technique. Look at your picking hand... are you using the correct picking (e.g. down and up – alternate)? Are you using the most appropriate fingers with your fretting hand?

3rd set of 10: **Memorize!**

Okay, time to try and memorize it. Don't be disheartened if you don't memorize it on the first go, that is what this set of 10 is for. Turn the page of music over and play without looking. This gives you a chance to focus on getting the notes flowing a bit more, or if you are already finding it easy, you can put more energy into it

4th set of 10: **Without Looking**

For the fourth set of 10, play the riff without looking at your picking hand. This enables you to get more used to the guitar. It is also great practice if you are wanting to sing and play, so that you can sing clearly without looking down at your guitar all of the time. If this is easy, you can try not looking at your fretting hand.

5th set of 10. **No Mistakes**

For the last set of 10, you should try and play a set of 10 without any mistakes. This may not always be possible right away but give it a go.

Exercise 4.6 Set Your Benchmark Lick!

Once you have used my 50X Method to get your favourite arpeggio, riff, lick or ostinato sounding great, you will have a greater sense of self-discipline. Now that you can practice something 50 times in a row, DO NOT go back to only 10 or 20 repetitions.

If you were a gymnast and you finally mastered 2 back flips in a row, you would not go back to practicing just one. Take the same approach with guitar practice. Use the new level/amount of times as a *benchmark*. Set your personal benchmarks and don't fall back from that. Set your goals, keep focused and let nothing stand in your way.

. . .

Extra Tip: Turn the page of your tablature or notation over before you think you have it mastered. Too often students use the sheet of music as a security measure when they could actually memorize it much sooner if they just tried.

My benchmark licks are:

Piece of music _____ Benchmark _____

Piece of music _____ Benchmark _____

Piece of music _____ Benchmark _____

Piece of music _____ Benchmark _____

Piece of music _____ Benchmark _____

Exercise 4.7 Always Go Over The Basics!

The best sports players do not always use fancy moves and techniques.

More often than not they will use the basics, but they will execute them better than beginners or amateurs because they have practiced them more, and they use them in a smarter way.

Being able to do this requires practice of the early basic techniques and moves that they learned. A similar balance between old and new is needed for musicians. One must learn new things of course – it keeps it interesting and it is useful to grow your knowledge base, but it is important that you really understand the principle of 'getting better at what you already know'.

Revision provides an opportunity to see what you have learned in a new light, especially as you look back with more experienced eyes, and it is simply a good exercise for strengthening your 'muscle memory' too.

This week, take time to go over everything you learned since you started learning how to play the guitar, and revise over every exercise of this course, starting at Exercise 1.1

Go over your notes in your 'What I Learned' notebook and put some physical practice of lessons learned into action.

Do not rush this – your progress with your guitar playing should not be rushed and it is best to understand thoroughly, and be able to play simple things well, rather than trying too much too soon.

Take your time, make time, be patient and have fun seeing how far you have come from the days of not knowing what a pick was!

Exercise 4.8 Improve Your Memory

Important: If you think you have a bad memory you will need to fix that thought straight away before you even touch the guitar again.

Not many with healthy minds have a bad memory unless they believe that they do.

. . .

Once you change your belief, you can train your memory like anything else. Start telling yourself that your memory is getting better and begin to put that into action by putting more time into memorizing songs.

Feed your brain with positive information coupled with action and your results on the guitar will improve also.

. . .

Remember: Play it once you'll probably forget it. Play it 10 times and you might remember it. Play it a thousand times and you can't forget it!

If you can't remember it you simply haven't played it enough times.

Once you have a piece of music memorized, then you can put more energy into getting the music flowing and making it sound good.

Repeat this phrase to yourself ten times: "Memorize to make it better".

Memorize to make it better. Memorize to make it better.
Memorize to make it better. Memorize to make it better.
Memorize to make it better. Memorize to make it better.
Memorize to make it better. Memorize to make it better.
Memorize to make it better.

Memorize to make it better!

How This Chapter Will Help You

Often people know what they want to improve but they don't know where to begin to seek advice. If you lack the funds to get a teacher immediately, this chapter will give you resources to start you on improving all the way to professional level if that's what you want.

The resources mentioned can also improve the skills of those who are already professional.

Interview Between Ryan Kershaw & Marty Shwartz

RK: People look at you and you know you're a successful teacher now, but I think for them it might be easy to think that it's always been easy. People might think as a teacher that you never had to struggle to put your finger on the fret properly or, you know, put your fingers around a chord but we know that the true story behind (every guitarists progress) - it's a little different.

MS: That's true.

RK: I'm sure you had a few challenges to overcome when you first started playing.

MS: I remember those first lessons I took when I was thirteen, there was just no connection to the stuff that we worked on for the first month of lessons. I just immediately thought the whole thing was just cumbersome and hard.

RK: Yeah.

MS: Everything about it. He didn't show me a chord or a power chord or even say what rock could – rock and roll could be.

Nothing about it was easy and it just, I didn't look forward to going but then when I was eighteen in high school, I was just starting to mess around harmonica and I had friends who played guitar so I was in a friendly environment. Teenagers, friends, you know - the high school kinda thing and I was just actually getting in there being able to jam on harmonica with these great guitar players. I was able to slowly get involved that way and then by just being the guitarist being casually there, you know. Of course anyone that doesn't play the guitar and I'm sure you know this one as well - of course they're going to grab a guitar and start (mucking around). People like to hold a guitar or sit on the couch and play with the guitar… epecially people that don't play! It just looks cool you know. So through that casualness I just learned a D chord. So instead of taking a formal lesson where I had a whole bunch of stuff in an hour, I just kind of like slowly got that D chord down so instead if I went to sit on a couch and grab someone's guitar instead of just nothing there, I could play D and go [demonstrates] and then I found out that I could do the 'sus' with my pinky or take my middle finger off. So I remember just the ease of guitar came when it was just comfortable, psychologically and tiny little bites of things you know. Just enough and then well hey, for instance I learned the D chord first right, and I could get it. I'd have to sit there and that finger, ok that finger, that finger ok. –

RK: So it's not like you just picked up the guitar and went oh D, sweet. You had still had to work on your fingers…

MS: Exactly. So yeah that was over a longer a time when that was my sit on the couch chord with my friend's guitar. But then once that got more comfortable, just by accident putting my pinky down I was like "Dude, that sounds so like Stairway to Heaven and like Tom Petty whatever like I can hear that". Then I could go [demonstrates]. Then ooh middle finger coming off! So just the ease of it made all the difference and then it was like, "dude that wasn't *that* hard you show me one other chord". Now I could do all my cool D stuff but go to another chord to just mix it up a little bit. So I did an A chord. And then also A and D was like, I found out there were already a bunch of songs I liked, and I was like "oh shit well maybe I should just find a third chord". So I'd say playing single notes and melodies and things were very hard but just learning a few chords that I could play something familiar right away gave me the motivation to keep learning just little bits.

RK: One of the things for beginner guitarists I find is that quite often they're afraid of just experimenting. Or I say "Come up and show me your own chord, make something up". And the natural reaction a lot of the time is I can't. Whereas of course you know that you can. I if you're scared to try things because it's going to sound bad it can slow you down. So what you're saying is quite cool in that "OK, I just did a D but then you went hey what happens if I put my finger here, or..."

MS: Right, right. Oh I was always like that. Just growing up too I leaned toward all artistic things whether it's creative writing, so you know coming up with my own stories, lots of imagination – things were related to imagination. Being in other places in my mind a lot, but I just always gravitated towards coming up with things on my own so it – like legos, art, any kind of art, stories, imagination, all that stuff – was just – that's the thing that I think I was natural at. It wasn't – I don't think I was musically – I think anyone can be capable of it but my strength was always like, if I learned three chords I'd made up my own I'd have a song. Or if I learned a scale I would just immediately start trying to come up with melodies, you know I'd just always have that creating my own thing with it. So that was not musical ability but it's like even now that the San Francisco stuff that I was in, that music is heavily improv'd. They kinda thrive on that Grateful Dead thing, and I just have always catered to that - being able to just have no plan and just start playing you know, I mean I love that. It's jazz related. But … yeah that was one thing that I was always doing and I'd seen other people and even other teachers, maybe some teachers that are way more teach in a technical way where it's more like you can tell that it's more of an engineer's mind, and that's just not me and I know there's some people that prefer that and I totally accept that is part of it so I'm kind of – but I'm grabbing onto the biggest niche, so one of the reasons why I do mostly beginner stuff is that if you look at my – all you have to do is look at my analytics to see that what the most popular stuff is is always the easy, acoustic, three-chord kind of pop songs. I mean obviously you have the classics, like, you know *Black Hole Sun* or *Sweet Child of Mine* or whatever, I mean those are always going to be humungous, Stairway to Heaven and everything - but for consistency it's always the Top 40, three-chord, easy acoustic songs.

RK: Yeah and that's something I say to my students a lot is don't go out and try and learn 50 new chords because just learning new things, new things, new things or new shapes - it's just learning facts and figures and there's no point in learning all the facts and figures if you can't understand what you're doing. So it's better just to get three chords but learn how to play them really, really well. Oh the other thing too is you mentioned *improv*, so just for guitarists who don't know the term – what do you mean by improv?

MS: The word *improvise* means to 'make up on the spot' - I think is the easiest simple definition. When you're improvising music you're really taking tools you have and improvising how you're using the tools that you've already worked on. So let's say you know a D chord, I mean in the simplest terms let's say you know a D power chord, and an A power chord. Just those two power chords is all you know right. Well improvising with those chords could be going OK I'm going to just start playing rhythms with these chords that I know with know plan of like how I'm going to do it so I could like be going A A AAAA AA D AAAAAAAA AA D you know I didn't know I was going to do that or even fling that to you until right then, I'm making it up as I go and it's an adventure, so you may go to a chord that sounds like crap, but you'll never know unless you're just letting it come right, and the thing that's the most addictive to me with music is uh, and I'm sure people will experience this when they do let's say meditation or when they do chanting, something happens sometimes, it's what you're always searching for. For me it's when you're improvising sometimes you reach this point, doesn't always happen when you reach a point when you don't feel like you're actually the one controlling it. Sometimes it feels like it's controlling you. And it's a, it's a higher consciousness that you can sometimes reach that you'll never get by playing a song that you've practiced and worked out from start to finish, every note's worked out how you're going to play it. And in the professional setting in music you have to be able to do that as well. It's probably more important to be able to do that, but when we're talking about improvisation I mean that's my favourite thing which I think relates to me using my imagination all the time growing up. That'swhere I always excelled as opposed to logic and math and science and things like that. Even though music is math, but the creative part of the tools is what I've always been drawn to.

RK: With improvisation, beginners can often get scared of learning scales though you don't have to go and learn a million but maybe one or two. Learn the pentatonic and the major scale. And so, your advice might be to do that – you know just to get a couple of scales down because they help you select notes that don't sound crap really…

MS: Yeah. I think so. I think in most settings of the music that I like and teach, I would try and get pretty competent in just main minor pentatonic scale because if you get good at that, where you actually have some vocabulary and chops, it shouldn't be that hard to start getting the other shapes. As opposed to learning all the modes up and down before you can actually create music right away, I think that's counterproductive.

RK: You have *Guitar Jamz* booklets and that on your site as well.

MS: Yeah, yeah.

RK: I was checking out that. They have a few of those things we just mentioned - the blues scale and pentatonic.

MS: Yeah, yeah. I keep it simple. Tthe main focus is all that YouTube stuff, keeping people engaged all the time and building a following and then the way smaller amount actually goes to that stuff which is like more focussed on the beginning of the business, creating all the products that I would sell. So it's kind of – it's an interesting thing - yeah, I almost consider my job as like the guy on YouTube you know, but I have to have a conversion to convert a percentage of all that into this funnel that gets really small and then they buy that stuff that you were showing me you know.

RK: So if beginners check out your YouTube stuff what's the best to start with?

MS: Yeah I mean honestly like really is to just, you can get a two-week free membership to the site.

RK: Oh yeah.

MS: Yeah, and you can just get on there and they're all lined up so you can kind of like start at square one and start go "OK I know that, next video. OK I know all that, next video." And then you can probably reach a point somewhere where you're like "OK this is where I'm going", and when you find that spot you can just keep going in the chronological order. I just focus on those main pentatonics in the beginning for a long time.

RK: 'Playing fast' is something that always comes up. Beginners want to play as fast as possible but quite often, OK ten times out of ten, if you try and play too fast the notes are going to sound crap, so –

MS: Oh yeah.

RK: So, uh what's your advice for beginners say that want to speed up but hopefully don't want to sound like shit. [laughter]

MS: Yeah, I mean I'm in that boat – I wish I played fast – I wish I could play my ideas faster, you know … So I'm in that boat as well, but what in my videos I actually literally slow down the video for when I say "To play fast you have to practice suuuupeeeeer slooooow." But it is true and I've seen so many amazing musicians say that, that I just have to believe that it's true that you gotta practice that articulation really slow. I was going to San Francisco, I was kind of getting an introduction into the scene that I wanted to be more involved in. It was my first foot in the door for that. So I really wanted to be on top of my chops and everything and so I what I did was, I had a metronome on my phone, you know a 'clicker.' So basically I've got this metronome and I would find just the right tempo to practice with, just scales. Maybe I would practice a scale sequence, maybe I'd improvise a little bit and do another thing, this and that. But basically I found the tempo that was too, just a *little bit* fast for me to alternate every picking consistently. So I just found whatever that was for me, to when I could still play but just, just that much faster. Just that much too fast, and then I would just practice everything to that and uh, for a long – you know all week. And it really played off actually. I don't know – I don't think I got faster but it just, it puts you there right. But then you gotta slow it down to where it's way comfortable no matter how, right. So for me it was like, 140 was pretty fast for me just to be blazing through all my blues stuff with all alternate picking. So I did that a lot, then I went down to 110 and did all the same stuff and felt like a champion. And then went right back up to 140 again you know and maybe I'd go up to 170 and just feel like how crazy that feels!

RK: Just to go nuts. [laughter]

MS: Yeah yeah, I'd like go wow that's impossible you know. And then how did Joe Bonamassa do that! [laughter]

RK: I remember I used to put on Iron Maiden and just try and shred over the top when I didn't even know a pentatonic was … some of it was cool but –

MS: Start with that, I mean that's a part of it too. I did a lot of playing along with stuff that I couldn't play at all you know. I don't know. There's something fun about that. Especially when you're younger, you know. It's kind of that imagining I was up on stage with those guys you know.

RK: Yeah and if you can crank it to 11 on the volume it seems to work a little bit better.

MS: It works a lot better yeah! I like that a lot. Love it. One of my favourite teachers when I said that to him he just said playing fast is not important. It means nothing to me, you know. It's more being proficient in your ideas. And if those ideas have to be fast then, then it should be important to you. But it's not like the be all end all. I play a lot less notes than I used to and that's all from musician's I respect critiquing me you know.

RK: Yup.

MS: It's hard though when you're up doing a gig the adrenaline makes you play a lot more notes. It's really hard to avoid it for me. It's a big problem.

RK: Sh – shaking's good for tremolo though. [laughter]

MS: Yeah yeah yeah. For sure, for sure man. Well on that While My Guitar Gently Weeps is one of those songs I got to – I got to do the solo on and you know it's got those big slow vibratos that he does in the intro that solo. So that was pretty cool I could just be still and my nerves were making it perfect.

RK: Yeah. And we were just saying man that for those people reading this that, weren't hearing our previous conversation, that you played at San Francisco – was it a couple of weeks you said?

MS: It was just last weekend. I just got back.

RK: Yeah so I mean for us even though we're teachers and we absolutely love teaching, I'm sure it's the same with you man - we have to *play* as well.

MS: Yeah man I think it pretty important. You can still be the best guitar teacher in the world and never play I think uh, it just depends on what it is you're doing; but I know for me personally I wouldn't be the guitar teacher I was if I hadn't done thousands of gigs as well. Because it's just the big picture as a musician. Especially on the mentoring front if you really know the ins and outs of the whole deal I think it just gives you perspective. You know like I said I mean all the guitar teachers I had were pretty well-known players. They were pretty respected and very busy as performers and played so I just consider it all the same thing. I never differentiated myself from musician to a guitar teacher, in fact most of my musician life until the last 7 years I always considered myself a guitar player and my day job was teaching guitar. I still consider it all one thing. There's this guy that I became friends with named Snuffy Walden and he's one of the most successful TV composers, but he's a guitar player. And, once again personal relationships led him and talent but all those friendships and connections through all the years led him to where his now which is this big composer but he goes out and gigs. He said his composing has been way better because he went out and starting gigging more because you just don't want to feel like you're in a hamster wheel. I've had that as a teacher where I've had to teach so much that it was just like every lesson was like rolling into the next lesson… so I think playing helps give you perspective of why you're doing it and how it all fits into your life.

RK: Yes. Especially when you're doing one on one tuition and it's no breaks in between. So on a beginner level I suppose … to get out and jam just do it as soon as you can really. It's not like you need to get to some magic level and then "oh I'm ready to jam." I remember thinking that when I was young and I was like "I don't know if I want to go into a band because I'm not good enough and I'm not…" – We can compare ourselves too much to other people, which is going to kill it. So, would you say the same? Just get out and if you're learning just play with other people just jam…

MS: Yeah, I mean that one's so hard because so much of that has to do with your personality too and who you are as like a individual. Some people are just so shy, that they may get enjoyment out of playing by themselves, and that's as far as they want to go. I think that's okay. It might help someone get confidence to eventually actually want to play with other people so I think part of it is, it could be a psychological thing for different personalities. But anyone that's wanting to play in a band or that fantasise about that - then they should do it right away. I've always told people to try. It's not always easy, but it's never been easier with the Internet to try and find people that are just a little bit better than you. It's always the best. Always the best. I've always had that and always benefitted from it. And be open to learn from anybody. With music, there can be all kinds of egos and stuff and I've seen that hurt people from growing who were maybe good when they were a teenager but … but that was it. A lot of people passing by you know. They didn't mature so, know I guess I'd have to put it in the categories. Like if you're fantasy is to play in a band, then you find someones friend that's doing the same thing man and just go for it. I mean some of the most famous bands were not great players and just started jamming in a garage and ended up becoming superstars. You've also got to play a lot to keep getting better.

RK: Did you find it with yourself as you were starting to jam with people… did you ever feel not so confident?

MS: I performed in front of the whole high school almost immediately when I started learning harmonica. Uh not by myself though. So we're talking you know 2,000 kids out in the centre of lunch time and I was just playing harmonica and I was just ready to do it man I was just so ready to get a girlfriend because I was a rockstar you know.

RK: [laughter]

MS: I was you know. I was eighteen dude I was ready to find that perfect angle you know to – to ah – to get – no it was super fun and I mean the funny thing is I should've been way more nervous coz I wasn't very good, but that's what you get when you're eighteen. I was more cocky so I just went for it. I probably got more nervous later as I actually got better and the situations changed, but I was doing improv comedy already at that point for fun. That's where personality is related to it because if you think about The Edge from U2, how different he is from someone like Jimi Hendrix.

RK: What made you pick up the harmonica?

MS: Well you know the funny thing was … I saw this band Blues Traveller open for Santana in, maybe 1991.Up to that point I was mostly into classic rock, so I liked Jimi Hendrix and Led Zeppelin and the Rolling Stones and the Beatles and Bob Marley and Sly and the Family Stone and the Grateful Dead and Lynyrd Skynyrd. I liked the Red Hot Chili Peppers and Nirvana and Guns N' Roses… all that as well, but when I saw Blues Traveller open for Santana they seemed like a band that were from a different era because they were improvising, jamming and the guy was just shredding on harmonica. It just made an impression on me. They're not my favourite band but I was at an impressionable age and I'd never heard of them before, and they seemed like a band that should've been from that other era from the seventies or something. I just saw 'em do it and then I bought their albums, and I was just really fascinated with it and then ... two of my best friends were great at guitar. When they would jam I was so jealous, you know friendly jealous but like just like – you know when you see two guys jam and you're just like... I wanted – from years before I always saw two guys jamming on guitar or a guy playing at a restaurant – anything, I always wanted to do it. So having two of my best friends actually jamming a blues jam I thought "Shit man, I could probably get a harmonica which is only twenty bucks and maybe figure it out and if not then no big deal. So it was that. It was really just wanting to jam so bad and not thinking I could – like guitar would be too hard, so I bought a cheap harmonica and just learned a few licks.

[*plays a bit of harmonica*]

You know. Still I still mess with it. But literally it was just a couple of fake blues licks and then all of a sudden you're now jamming with them, I'm at like these rehearsals where guitars are all around - so I could grab a guitar and start playing that D chord I was talking about. Harmonica was my way to play with my friends as fast as possible, and logically to me seemed like getting a harmonica was the way to go.

RK: That's what we're saying eh man just get a couple of chords or whatever. Just get *something* and just get in and try it and have a go.

MS: Yeah and I was so confident, I wasn't even playing the right key man! it sounded completely wrong but I was just selling it you know. And people wouldn't even say I was really good and I wasn't even in the right key so what does that tell you!

RK: (jokes) Yeah well a few whiskeys usually loosens that up and it kinda slips it in the right key somehow.

MS: Yeah it does. Have every fourth song just accidentally is in the right key and all of a sudden – "Whoa, let's do that one again! That was a good one remember that one yeah that was really good you know. But then I just started – you know it was this tiny little, tiny little steps man like I swear when I knew like three chords on guitar I was just like that's all good, I'm never gonna like solo, I'm never going to play electric guitar, I just want to be able to sing some songs to some girls when the time is right if need be and uh, and I was like yeah I'll learn that one extra chord but I'll never do the barre chords just show me open chord songs and I'm good. All right show me that one B minor chord I'll work on it a little bit then that's that. All right show me another one OK cool. You know and it was just like one thing after the next and uh, all right I'm never going to solo but just – just show me that one thing right there, that little lick thing you know I don't care about the scale just show me that lick. All right what scale does that lick come from. OK I will – OK I'll just play it a little bit. Hey that sounds pretty good you know like it was just like – and then when I went to college I was not going to college for music, it was my hobby and I was like well I met some cool guitar players who were better than me, so I played with them all the time. I started to get almost as good as them. But I would never major in music or do music for a job you know I was just going to get better because I loved it so much and then I was like OK, I heard there's a good guitar teacher here at this college so I'm going to take it as an elective just so I can get better. And then all of a sudden I got way better, you know because he was a great teacher so it just kind of found me you know it just never ended. And then that guitar teacher was uh ... I mean he was kind of like as far as I was idolising his life was – looked awesome to me like, he taught at the college, was super fun and he taught more intermediate players so it wasn't like you know baby sitting, uh he played in a band that played all around, he had a cool, you know cool apartment a really hot girlfriend, looked very comfortable in life you know, I was like dude if I could do that, then you can always like try to be a rock star or famous or whatever that like ultimate dream is but like I could do that then like what my teacher's doing. He's making $300 a week just with the band and then you know I don't know what else with the teaching but – but he was comfortable you know. So I kind of thought you know that's a – that's a better way than like getting a shitty job. If I could like maybe work that angle I think I'm a people person I think I can do it. And so what happened was, my junior year of college, that guitar teacher decided he was playing out too much he wanted to be home more or whatever so he quit the band and put a word in for me to audition to take his place. So, uh I got the gig. And so my – before I graduated college I was able to pay my rent and live just with this nice little weekend gig cover band playing lots of funk from the seventies with all older guys. So it was just a great like learning experience too. Uh but yeah so what happened to me was I was able to like support myself before I finished school. And uh, so I just kinda cruised on that for a while. But then the problem is you don't ever make any more money, so like 5 years ago like you're still making that $300 a week, all of a sudden it's not as attractive coz there's no growth. And so you know I just eventually got to the point – [inaudible] in, what's called New Mexico, which is in the southwest near Colorado, Texas, kind of mountainy, snow and mountains in the winter but really nice desert and sunshine in the uh summer and spring. But it's a really small town that I was in. So I was just kind of a big fish in a small town and – the woman that's now my wife was my girlfriend and you know I just had the perfect life for a twenty two year old or whatever. And then you know eventually you get a little bit older and I'm like OK if I'm really ever gonna find out if I made the most of my musical talent that I've worked on here if I ever really ah … want to see if I can really give it it's all then I've got to go back to the – California. So I moved to California in uh … in '98. Got engaged to my wife and uh all that and – I'm from California so I'm kind of just back – moved back home.

RK: So the guitar thing of attracting the right girl it uh didn't work out too bad for ya. [laughter]

MS: No before my wife I mean it was always the – I mean let's face it. It's the best, it is the best tool I had in my toolbox let's put it that way. And I always talk about – it's a joke but it's also a true story like, the bottom line Marty why did you – what made you want to learn guitar. And I always tell a story of a bit little bit earlier in high school when I went to this high school party, and this dude was playing the Mr Big song I'm The One Who Wants To Be With You. He's playing it on acoustic guitar and he was just surrounded by girls. Like he was in the middle of the mushpot, as they call it in duck duck goose he was in the mushpot surrounded by chicks and they were all like singing and like swaying and were like literally rock star like ...

RK: That's really a Spinal Tap – it's a perfect song for that situation. [laughter]

MS: Well yeah he had blond blond hair and he was just like [inaudible] hair and you know and uh, like Robert Plant hair you know whatever but ah, but you know the chicks were just going crazy for him and I just remember thinking to myself – dude! Ah! I need that, I need that, so that's always a good motivation honestly I mean you've gotta – it's so hard to do music like professionally. You have to love it way more than for the chicks man." I mean you gotta you gotta love it so much. I'm just trying to do it as a job, right. Anyone can play guitar and get tons of enjoyment out of it. But I'm saying to have music as a career is so ... the odds are stacked so against it, that you just have to love it so much that you're willing to do it for free and if you can so happen to make a living doing it - then all the better! It's hard to come to terms with that ... but you know I had to come to terms with it before Guitar Jamz was successful for me.

RK: And did you find that it actually freed you up to just get on with it and do it? Because it's great having goals and that's something I teach. But at that same time if you're so focussed on the goal that you're not enjoying what you're doing at the moment it just doesn't work. If you can free yourself up a bit and realise that you've got to do what you love first and foremost it makes everything else come a bit easier and a bit better doesn't it.

MS: It does, and again Guitar Jamz happened right after I made the decision that I really wasn't going to pursue it as my full time career any more. I will always have my talent; I will always have my ability to play so if something does come along that's the right thing then I'm ready to do it and I'm totally capable to do it, but I really need to pursue – you know I was already really into the education thing, but I mean I was at that point when I was ready to not do it as my career because yeah, it takes the enjoyment out of it you know like, I would rather enjoy – start enjoying it again then be burning out and not getting anywhere, so yeah. Yeah. For sure.

RK: Cool. Talking about your sites too man. So you've got Guitar Jamz and you've got your YouTube channel. Beginners could check out your YouTube first?

MS: The featured video that I have on YouTube is like you're – it's called your absolute super beginner first guitar lesson, something like that. Maybe the words are switched around on that but it's definitely something that starts with absolute super beginner first guitar lesson you know those are in there. And if you go there I break it down to literally "if you got one finger that worked and two strings on a guitar, this is where we're going to start and don't be scared - everyone started here." that's probably your best first lesson. You know I don't know I – I don't even care I think uh, I'm kind of like harder not to find out there than I am to found if you into guitar so really I would say try and not find me and see what comes up.

RK: [laughter]

MS: And then tell me what comes up coz I think you're going to find me anyway. Yeah I know that some other guitar teachers probably have a problem with that I apologise. Uh, I didn't do any uh, all I did was make a lot of videos my style. I didn't pay for any of those hits or anything. It's all organic.

RK: it's really cool though and it's good to see another guitar player out there doing it. With this interview I wanna – it's for beginners to check out, but just in terms of guitar teachers and that as well I think it's cool just to be happy for other people seeing them do well. How I relate that to beginners is quite often they get worried about playing in front of people that are gunna judge them or if they're better than them, but I always say to my students "If you go to a show and people are – especially experienced guitarists are knocking you down, then you're jamming with the wrong people."

MS: Yeah, for sure. I agree and unfortunately there's just – with guitar there's a lot of that out there. But some of the best musicians I have ever seen were the most humble and also totally unknown. I've had people blow my mind that maybe they're known in that city or whatever, but I mean I've seen guys that have just absolutely blown my mind that are not famous or anything, so fame and all that is not always related to quality and happiness either really.

RK: Amen to that.

MS: Yeah. But yeah I mean, any field in your life if someone's knocking down they're the wrong person right.

RK: Yeah fully. Yeah.

MS: With music I've been around a long time and seen that there are a lot of artists and performers that have something broken, you know and they're trying to fix it with attention from the audience. And they're going to knock another person down that's affecting them because something is broken in there you know, so. I don't know - it's heavily psychological in the arts. People like that are kinda driven to it. There's a lot a going on, you know. Being in San Francisco around so many musicians there's all these different band dynamics and dramas that go on that are almost impossible to avoid.

RK: That's a whole other book as well. [laughter]

MS: That's another uh, that's another library!

RK: That's when you just gotta pick up your guitar and jam. [laughter]

MS: Yeah I mean you know being married to one person's difficult enough but you know a band is almost impossible.

RK: Yeah.

MS: Bam. You know. Just depends.

RK: Hey man we'll just got a couple more and then I'll let you shoot coz I know you're busy so, one of the things that I've seen on one of your videos you're talking to Robben Ford

MS: Yeah.

RK: - who's a great guitarist and an influence on you.

MS: Oh yeah man he's one of my favourite players. For sure yeah. I helped him put a couple of clinics together for himself. I don't know what happened I think his manager reached out to me because he does some guitar lesson stuff. I was so excited, I was just hoping I'd maybe get a couple of one on one lessons with him and so I was just falling down my rabbit's hole with the manager thinking in the back of my head "Well I can probably help him and maybe he can be my Obi Wan Kenobi" you know, but uh yeah I just – it didn't work out that way. He's not really that kind of guy. But I helped put some clinics together and did a couple of interviews and – you know just plugged. I was just trying to help him coz I admire him as a guitar player. He's not my mentor or anything - that's what I was kind of hoping when I first like was in contact with them - but that's another lesson too. Things aren't always what you're going to imagine them to be, so you have to have that openness to something going either way. He's amazing and he's so awesome. He plays in one of those Dumble amps, you know that are like $150,000 per amp but only a few guys have them, so he's got this holy grail amplifier. I'd say more than anything I just love his guitar playing.

RK: Yeah.

MS: Yeah. Do you listen to him?

RK: Little bits and pieces yeah not for a while though…

MS: The thing I especially love is the way he solos; he's super tasty. His phrasing is just sophisticated enough but it's always got soul and blues in it, and that's just what I like. I don't like super crazy jazz... I like stuff that's bluesy, and I think he does that really well. Larry Carlton is like that as well and those two guys are friends they do gigs together a lot. So I definitely like that style. But yeah dude, that guy Robben Ford's one of the best I think.

RK: There's an English guitar magazine Guitar Techniques...

MS: Yeah.

RK: They're really good for supporting Robben's stuff and for years I'd see Robben Ford in every second one so.

MS: Yeah it's interesting you know a lot of that stuff goes back once again to like personal relationships like someone that he's friends with or that he's just friends with that company through various years and connections. Honestly, Europe is way better for blues, than America... and Japan too. I've never been to Japan. I'd love to go there but yeah so that would make sense coz you're saying that's a – was it UK magazine?

RK: Yeah...

MS: Yeah so that makes sense - they love the blues. I was there with Justin (Sandercoe), and we got to do some playing and stuff there.I've gigged there with this guy like over ten years ago like from American Idol so I've played there before, but I'd love to go over there really as myself and do something. There's more appreciation for it. I don't know if there's the hustle and bustle here. People don't want to hear a band they'd rather do something else. But ... it's all good. I've got my computer screen so I can reach people.

RK: Cool; OK man - last one brother.

MS: Alright...

RK: If you've got three bits of advice for beginner guitarists. What would you say?

MS: Three bits of advice... I guess I would start with three shapes. Three shapes can play a million songs that you recognise. So if you think about how hard it is in the beginning just remember that those three shapes are actually for millions of songs so that first little hump; it's not just to be able to play one song with how hard those chords are in the beginning or how awkward it feels. That first investment is for the rest of your easy song career. That's why people give up in the beginning: it's just that first hump. That first hump! Number one, be patient in the beginning. Uh, you know obviously if you be patient for the whole thing, good. But I mean I just need to stick with it especially in the beginning. Learn the open easy chords and learn a bunch of songs with those first. Don't get carried away if you get a song that seems too hard, don't learn it yet. Learn an easier one. You'll be surprised like let's say take a song because it's too hard for you, you can learn - if you go for it right, way too hard, now you have a mental crutch against that song because it's got that power chord or whatever. Instead you should go back and pay super easy songs. Get 'em all down, go back to that and you will find it's easier because this was just mileage on your – on your engine you know. Muscles building. So each – you could take – learn four songs with the same three chords but recognise them as four separate songs. Then go for that one that's a little bit harder. If you get to a song that's way too hard for you it's the wrong song to be learning. You want a song that's just a little bit of a challenge.

RK: So just to clarify Marty so Stairway to Heaven not on the first lesson?

MS: No. Absolutely not, unless uh, unless it's like, yeah... Let's just say no.

RK: [laughter]

MS: I was going to say unless you're like playing a little melody with like one finger or something but let's just – oh cut – here's the reason why. The reason I paused was because I told you the first thing I knew for like a year was just the D chord. I could go [demonstrates] I knew that was from Stairway to Heaven so, so that's why I'm saying you almost want to say 'no' you know. I like in the beginning just hoppin around man with all those easy chords. So, patience with yourself in the beginning and then learn all the super basic open chords and play lots of easy songs and that's what I would start with. I think that's – yeah I think that's – because really, I mean the only other option for number three is to stay inspired. Musically. As a music fan. So that's probably better I'd say. So I'd say patience with yourself in the beginning, just start with the open easy chords and lots of easy open chord strummers, and this one [laughter] which I go like that with my uh, when I'm using my middle finger for a thing on the thing I go like that coz it's offensive here, (middle finger pointed up) uh … see now I'm using my humour and getting distracted. So what was it it was staying passionate as a music fan.

RK: Learn the basic chords and flip the –

MS: Coz I always flip the bird man. You know all the punk rockers do that in their pictures. So now it's cliché actually but, yeah so patience with yourself in the beginning, all the easy open chords, stay passionate as a music fan. Staying passionate as a music fan was the biggest thing for me in the beginning because I was that teenager that was listening to all the favourite bands. The internet didn't exist yet or you know we didn't all have the internet yet so, it was something that I was super into. Listening to my favourite bands, studying about them, looking at the liner notes listening to my favourite albums in my car. It was a big part of the teenager thing - all my favourite bands that I connect to with my life at that adolescent point. So when I actually started learning a few chords, some of those songs that were so important to me were actually super easy and blew me away. I just assumed they were not easy! A three chord song, I just assumed it wasn't that easy. So, yeah. I think that's it.

RK: Awesome man.

MS: Yeah man.

RK: OK well thanks Marty for the chat and some awesome advice for beginners. Hopefully we'll get a few people going to your site guitarjamz.com and check out the YouTube channel as well.

MS: Z, guitar jamz with a z. And, also there's this – there's this website, ah not everyone's heard of it but it's called YouTube. And you can go there and look up guitar lessons and there's a few videos.

RK: Oh yeah we get – we get that in New Zealand.

MS: Oh you do – you guys got that?

RK: Yeah we just got – we just got computers. [laughter]

MS: Well that's fantastic, so then that if everyone already knows about it you can go there and I've got a few videos on there with some guitar stuff so, feel free. And that is free. Totally free.

RK: Awesome.

MS: Yeah man, for sure. Is there anyone to say goodbye to out there. Anyone that reads this… thank you.

RK: There you go all the future jammers out there and future guitar legends!

Chapter 5 - Repeat and Memorize: Brainwash Yourself With Great Information

"Repetition is the mother of skill" - Anthony Robbins.

Why Repetition Works

An analogy I like to give to my students when talking about memorizing pieces or memorizing music is that it's like typing an email address; when you first start it might take you a while, especially if you've got a strange address and you have to look at where the keys are and it takes a bit of time to get to each letter. But after a while, you can type it in just a few seconds because you have typed the same thing over and over again. It works the same way with music; it's just commonsense.

People always say, "Oh I can't memorize it, or I'm having trouble memorizing the song." Without fail I ask them, "How many times have you tried the song through?" "Oh, I've tried it you know a few times." "Okay how many times?" "Oh, I had a go on Tuesday." Well that's not going to help you memorize it.

It's commonsense. Say a sentence once and you might forget it. Say it ten times you will probably remember it. Say it a thousand times and you can't forget it. Take this approach to playing. It doesn't matter how hard something is, you can do it. You just have to put the time in and do it enough.

People like things that are familiar to them and in the song by the Smashing Pumpkins, Billy Corgan says, "Love, love, it's who you know." Well similar with music; there's different ways to memorize. Derren Brown has an interesting technique for memorizing things using pictures in the mind. It might help you to memorize if you listen to a recording of someone teaching guitar, or it might help you if you visually look at something.

An option to aid in memorization is to think in patterns. One thing you can try when you're learning a piece of music, is to memorize four notes at a time, rather than just looking at one note, looking back down at the guitar and playing it, looking back up, playing the next note. Try groups of four. Work on bars or sections first. Don't just play and battle through one song over and over and over.

If you're hiking through the forest up a hill and it's a really steep hill, or a mountain, how would you do that? You would do it at intervals; you would hike up a little bit and then you'd stop, and then you'd hike up the next bit. The same tactic works with a hard song or solo; you try bits at a time.

Turn the page before you think you have to. This is an important step. Try and memorize one line of a song that you're playing. Turn the page over and see if you can play it without looking.

What most people will do is try and memorize it first and totally have it ingrained before they try turning the page over, but turn the page over before you think you have the song. Its part of the process of memorizing in that you will probably get a few notes wrong first, but that's fine, it's all part of it. Turn the page over before you think you have it and you might surprise yourself.

Hooks

A hook is something catchy that repeats and draws you into a song. It doesn't have to be the guitar, but for now because this is a guitar-focused book, we'll concentrate on the guitar.

You can have hooks in lead and rhythm. Don't just think that a hook is only for the chords of a song or a riff; **you can have hooks in solos as well**.

Some of the greatest songs are those that have a signature hook and a hook is just that, it's a signature to a song. If you think of songs that stand the test of time, like *Smoke on the Water* for example, da-da-dah-da-da-da-dah; everybody knows that riff from young people to grandmas and grandpas. We all know *Smoke on the Water* and it's because of that simple riff.

Simplicity is the key to hooks. I remember being in high school and I'd already been playing guitar for some years. I was sitting next to a friend and she had only been playing guitar about six months. She was playing *Smoke on the Water* and she said to me "It's like a telephone number – 0350365." I thought that was a great way to memorize something. I was trying to do all the technical sides of things and had overlooked such a simple idea because I was trying to look for the hard way of doing things. Simplicity works and it works for hooks.

Think about the great hooks - *Layla, You Really Got Me* by The Kinks, *Smoke on the Water* by Deep Purple, *and Iron Man* by Black Sabbath. They're all very, very simple and hooks are used in all styles of music. It doesn't matter what it is, I can guarantee that if you have a favorite song it most likely has an effective hook.

I would suggest reading about hooks some more and try and make up your own. I call a hook a 'Song's Logo'. ™

Giving Something the Same Rhythm Helps Memory

One thing that does help memory and memorizing things is rhythm. Example, think of your times tables - 2x2=4, 4x4=16, da-da-da-da-da; da-da-da-da-da. It's a song. A better example is probably the alphabet, ABCDEFG. Think about the alphabet song that you learnt when you were a child; it helps you because it has rhythm to it. ABCDEFG da-da-da-da-da-da-dah.

Try and memorize the rhythm of a song first by listening to it. If you don't know how the rhythm of a song goes in your head, it's going to be hard to physically play that.

Once you play something where you can get the rhythm smoothly, then it's easier to memorize. So don't expect to memorize something if you're still having trouble with the tune. The first step is to get the tune and then to play it enough so that you have it memorized. Knowing the rhythm and tune helps you to memorize.

My '50X Method' ™

Refer to the *Use Your Buzz* workbooks for my very effective 50X method to help you memorize pieces of music.

You can find my instructional video online, and get access to the bonus PDF at:
ryan-kershaw.teachable.com

Exercise 5.1 Put Memorization Into Practise

After re-reading Chapter 5 of *Use Your Buzz To Play The Guitar*, pick an easy song or section of a harder song and commit it to memory this week!

Song _____

Section _____

Make sure that the section has no more than 4 chords. If you choose a riff that uses single notes, try and find a riff that is limited to 8 notes.

Utilize my 50X Method for help with this exercise (visual recording available to view)

Exercise 5.2 Using Hooks In Improvisation

Let's get back to some improvisation. Using either the Major scale or the minor Pentatonic, play over an easy backing track you have used before, using the idea mentioned below.

What is a hook? Write the answer on the lines below and try to keep the answer as simple as possible.

A *hook* is:

_____

_____

_____

_____

_____

_____

_____

Tasks for Exercise 5.2:

1. Incorporate a hook into your improvisation. Keep the hook simple at first and between just 2 to 4 notes long.

2. Read two online articles about 'hooks in music'.

Exercise 5.3 Develop Your Patience

It might sound strange but the invisible qualities of a guitarist are often the most powerful. Traits like having good patience, a positive attitude towards learning and being able to incorporate self-discipline into practice are all beneficial to the player.

For this exercise I'd like you to work on your mental abilities and simply be aware of what frustrates you when you are practicing. The next step is to take note and simply fix the error or slow down rather than get annoyed.

For example, if you are trying a new chord but it isn't sounding clear; work out why it is not sounding clear. If a finger is accidentally resting on a string, shift it's position so that the chord becomes clear. This is a much better approach than becoming frustrated and also helps you to learn in the process.

Another way to develop your patience is to purposely slow-down on the final repetitions of an exercise. Most people will speed up because they know that they are near the end, but if you slow-down it strengthens your sense of control and patience.

How This Chapter will Help You

Rhythm and repetition are two of the most important components of practicing music.

Establishing the use of hooks in your material will make your playing stand out and **developing the discipline of repetition in practice will help you improve more quickly.**

Chapter 6 - Little Things Are The Biggest: The greatest secret of professional players

Little Things – Ryan Kershaw

Little things are funny things, they sit staring at the table side, like tiny guardian angels protecting me where my heart abides, and even though they refrain from being grand in actual size, the love in which they're given glows strong when happiness hides.

Little things like cats and dogs to others may look slight, but we both know what they mean when it's hard to feel the light.

And when Pearl went away it was you who was the only one that knew, how much I missed her dearly and how my heart was broken too.

Little things are precious and little things I keep, close to me when big things make me lose my sleep.

It's the little things you have given me that have always got me through, it's those little things that mean more to me nana, more than you ever knew.

~ ~ ~ ~

As in life, little things make the biggest difference. The most common misconception people have when learning how to play music is that if you learn lots of scales and you learn lots of chords you're going to be a good guitar player. That is the farthest thing from the truth.

If you learn more scales, you're just learning more notes. You need to learn the little things with them. You need to learn how to bend in tune when you need to.

Learn what different actions do for the strings. Learn why you play hammer-ons and pull-offs. Learn what artists do. Don't just learn more notes and scales; it's not going to do anything by itself.

Technique Substitution™

An example of technique substitution is bends instead of slides. Most players know what a slide is and they know what a bend is, but they don't really know why they're playing them or where to play them; they just play them randomly, if they think a bend should go there they'll chuck it in.

But think about what they do. A bend raises the pitch smoothly whereas a slide when you slow it down, you'll hear that fret bump as you go over the frets. So try if you've got a slow slide in a song, say *Albatross* from Fleetwood Mac, you can hear those really nice gentle slides.

Jeremy Spencer was using a guitar slide there but if you don't have a slide you can get by, with using a bend instead of a finger slide.

An example of a player who's really good at using subtle things and substituting techniques is David Gilmour from Pink Floyd. Listen to the string rake in the first solo of *Comfortably Numb*; the string rake as he just goes into that first note of the solo. It's such a small thing but it's so cool. It sounds much better than what most guitar players would do; just play the note on its own. The subtle things make the biggest difference.

Another little tidbit that you can use is being aware that the position of blocked strings affects the sound produced. Blocked strings aren't always random either; they can be the signature of a riff. An example is *Smells Like Teen Spirit* by Nirvana - those blocked strings in between the chords is a big part of that sound; or *Santa Monica* by Everclear is an even better example.

Where you put your hand on the strings affects what pitch the blocked strings make. Try blocking the strings up by the bridge of the guitar; it sounds different than if you put your hand way down by the headstock.

Knowing Why to Use a Technique

Again, I have mentioned this before, but knowing why to use a technique is so important. Knowing what the differences are of picking versus using hammer-ons.

What about the difference for using a palm mute. Most people just chuck their palm on the bridge and hope that it sounds okay. You can use varying degrees of palm muting. The further forward towards the neck you put your hand the more cut off the sound will be. You might just want a very slight palm mute; *listen to the differences.*

When a golfer plays golf, a slight turn, 5mm turn of the club, will make a big difference in the direction of the ball. In the same way, it's the small things that make the biggest difference in your playing an instrument.

Control over the small techniques means that you can do what is necessary to communicate the feel of the music more effectively. A good example of this is Kirk Hammett and his phrasing, or Tony Iommi who plays most of his songs on the thick strings; he doesn't play 'Paranoid' from the A string because the tone is different from the tone of the low E string.

Accents

As with speaking, it's not so much what you say, it's how you say it; and the same can be said for music.

You can play the same riff but give it a different feel by using subtle changes of timing, or accents, or palm mute. Try it; try playing the same rhythm over and over but putting an accent - and if you don't know what it an accent is, it is simply an emphasis on a certain note - try putting the accent on a different note of the riff.

Tone

Take time to sit down with an amp and sort out your tone. I remember playing a show and a friend asked, "How do you get that great tone; what pedals are you using?" I said, "I'm not using any pedals. I'm going straight through the amp," and he couldn't believe it.

But amps are made to sound good. It's just that most players don't take the time to learn all the different settings they can get out of it.

Read about simple things like treble, mid and bass. Try different amps; even if you can't afford one yet, there's nothing stopping you from going to a shop and trying one out. But don't just try it because you are in a shop and playing an amp; see what the differences are. Learn why you like a particular sound.

Different songs may suit different tones to each other, and it is good to be able to use different tones, just as it is useful to appreciate different styles of playing…

Exercise 6.1 Technique Substitution™

Chord substitution (putting a chord in another chords place that still fits the music) is common in music, but I coined the term 'Technique Substitution'.

Technique substitution is swapping one technique for another and is most often overlooked.

A great boxer not only knows how to punch, but they know why, and also know when to do a hook rather than a jab. In music you should know when a slide sounds more effective than a hammer. You can also delve deeper into the effect techniques produce and stylize a song or lick but using specific techniques.

Crafting a better understanding of techniques, and when and why to use them, will help you to gain control of your playing like a master sculptor has control of their tools.

1. Try swapping a bend for a slide (and the reverse) and note the differences in your 'What I Learned' notebook.

If you are not aware of what string bending is – that's O.K, don't panic – just take your time to research the technique online first and after you have practiced complete this exercise. If you are more advanced, try the same principle but with more advanced techniques, or a riff or lick that you like to play.

This might seem insignificant but please do not skip this exercise. It not only gets you using your creativity, but it also develops your ear and grows awareness of how the small things do have an affect.

Exercise 6.2 Blocked strings

Blocking your strings is a basic technique that should be in every guitarists 'technique inventory'. It is found in most styles of playing and in genres such as Reggae and Funk it even makes up a big part of the signature sound of those styles.

1. What is a 'blocked' string?

_____

_____

_____

_____

2. Practice using a blocked-string rhythm by placing your fretting hand over all of the strings. Using the up and down arrows, write down what strum patterns you used and remember them for other songs that you might make in the future.

3. Many guitarists do not know that if you shift the blocked strings along the neck, the sound will change – and you can actually use that to great effect for songs. If you have a four-chord song, you can start by playing the chords using blocked strings (release pressure on the notes but keep the fingers on the strings), and then go into the chords after that without applying the blocked strings.

What differences do you notice between playing blocked strings in different places along the fretboard?

Differences / What Happens:

Reminder: Remember to always write down everything that you learn in your 'What I Learned' notebook.

Exercise 6.3 The 'Palm Mute'

Another basic technique that every guitarist should be able to play well is the 'palm mute'. The blocked string technique is often called a *fret hand mute* but the palm mute is when you use the palm of your picking hand to mute the strings slightly. You should still be able to hear the tone of the strings, but they will sound dulled a little.

The technique is again found in all styles, though is especially prevalent in Metal and Surf genres.

1. What is a Palm Mute

_____

_____

_____

_____

2. How is a **palm mute** different to a **blocked string** and how could you use palm muting in your playing?

_____

_____

_____

_____

_____

_____

_____

3. All of the techniques and exercises in module 6 can be applied to licks and improvisation, not just riffs or chords. Put palm muting into your playing this week.

Ryans Tip: always think outside of the box, and try 'opposites'. So, if you learn something for a lead lick, try it for a rhythm riff too (and vice versa).

Exercise 6.4 The Hammer-On

The *hammer-on,* often referred to simply as the 'hammer', is perhaps the most common of the basic techniques. A hammer is similar to a 'slur' on the violin, where you play multiple notes with only one stroke of the bow, though in guitar this means playing two notes but only picking the first. You can also utilize more than one hammer in succession for more than two notes.

I won't give you the answer as to why it is used – you can find that out for yourself if you listen to my videos, but knowing *why* a hammer is used is important. Knowing the reasons or benefits behind the application of any technique is important as then you can know where to use it in the songs that you play.

1. What is a Hammer-on?

_____

_____

_____

_____

2. What is a Hammer-on used for?

_____

_____

_____

_____

3. Hammer Exercise:

Play a hamer-on, starting at the 5th fret on the thick string. After picking the note at the 5th fret with your first finger, hammer from your first finger to the next fret (fret 6) using your second finger. Repeat this on each string and work your way down to the thin string. Repeat this a minimum of 100 times every day this week.

Make sure that you do it a minimum of 100 times for this exercise to be effective, and stay disciplined. It exercises your mind and patience as much as it does your fingers.

Exercise 6.5 Accents!

When you talk, how you are heard is not just according to what you say but also the way you say it, and your *accent*.

In music, you play the notes and obviously what notes you play makes a difference, but *how you play them* can matter even more!

Accents are a slightly more advanced technique that all beginners should aim to master, where you emphasize certain notes, usually by increasing the volume or picking slightly harder. You can get a similar effect when releasing a palm mute.

Accents are another one of those small things that add expression and life to your playing, and jump in the bag with your other techniques to help you develop tools to express your own individual style on the guitar – so don't ignore them!

1. What is an accent? (Write down even if you already know the answer – revision is good and by writing things down it reminds you and processes in your mind on a deeper level)

   _____

   _____

   _____

2. Why would you use accents in guitar playing?

_____

_____

_____

3. Focus solely on using accents in your next 3 practice sessions. It is important to dedicate a good amount of time to getting your head and fingers around each technique. Do not ignore this step either – it is seemingly small but very important!

Exercise 6.6 Know Your Tone!

Great players have good technique, but also aim for great tone. Read about 'tone on acoustic instruments.'

1. What is tone?

_____

_____

_____

2. What are the tone controls on your guitar if you have them, and what do they do?

_____

_____

_____

_____

_____

3. What are the tone controls on your amp and what do they do? If you don't have an amp, use a guitar amp that you find online, or a friends amp as an example

_____

_____

_____

_____

_____

_____

_____

_____

Write your settings: Dial is function (e.g *treble*) Setting is number on amp (e.g '9' or '3'

Dial _____ Setting _____   Dial _____ Setting _____

Dial _____ Setting _____   Dial _____ Setting _____

Dial _____ Setting _____   Dial _____ Setting _____

Dial _____ Setting _____   Dial _____ Setting _____

Dial _____ Setting _____   Dial _____ Setting _____

How This Chapter Will Help You

This is a *really* important chapter for intermediate and advanced players.

The difference between intermediate level players and advanced guitarists is not determined by big things such as brand new scale shapes or chords, but by little things.

Realizing this and putting the 'musical microscope' on your playing will help you build the bridge from amateur to pro.

Chapter 7 - Appreciate Different Styles: Understanding Others Will Help You

"It seems like people get afraid of a certain music if they can't pigeon hole it to their satisfaction. Good music is good music and that should be enough for anybody." - Bradley Nowell of the band Sublime

Sports players learn from variety. The best of the best have different influences and they learn how those that influenced them to become the best.

In order to improve, it is strongly advised that you learn to appreciate different styles. It's important to realize that appreciating is not the same as loving. I used to not be able to differentiate between the two. When I was about eight years old, I was obsessed with Guns N' Roses and no other band came close. Since I didn't really understand the difference between 'appreciating' and 'liking', I couldn't appreciate a band that I didn't think was that good, even if it was the greatest band in the world. Now I realize that what I like and I think is the best band in the world might not be the best, but it's my opinion that the band is.

Appreciating different styles is a healthy thing. I am not a fan of hip-hop but I appreciate the fact that it has made a big difference to many people. The dictionary definition, or at least one dictionary definition of appreciate, is to understand the full value of. Do you think you could appreciate the Blues, for example, and see how the Blues led onto various forms of rock music - even if you're not a big fan of the Blues style? If you can do this you will learn a great deal and open your mind to many more possibilities.

A really fantastic idea and something I get my students to do often is to jam to styles of music other than what they are used to. It's easy to jam over the same old backing tracks; try something different. One track I recommend is *Dr. No's Fantasy*. It can be found on a great series of albums called the 'Ultra-Lounge Series' and it has these kind of cool Latin rhythms; percussive stuff going on with the congas and it's not just your four chord power chord type deal. It's so cool because you have to think differently than what you usually would, unless you play that style all the time anyway. But most of us would have to think differently to put the guitar over the top.

Another development exercise I teach is to jam over a song where there are 3 or more guitar tracks already included in the recording. That's actually a great thing to do; it really forces you to leave room for the other instruments.

You can always pick up on the basic points of different styles as well. For example, with Spanish guitar you might not be an expert and you might even not have a clue how to play in a Spanish style, but you can experiment and find out the trademarks of that style of playing.

For Spanish guitar, you might use 3rds. Go over the 3rds in C again, which means you run up a C scale and add a 3rd to each note, and incorporate some tremolo picking. Again, if you don't know what tremolo picking is, look it up.

Use string raking, use the natural minor scale. Find out what scales are signatures of each style. Experiment with chromatic ideas; use trills or minor second pull-offs. Based around the keys of A and E, find what keys are really used predominantly in different styles.

For a Spanish style of guitar, you might use body strikes or incorporate open major scales. Try and find these kinds of trademarks of these different styles of playing.

Sometimes these things can be unexpected too. Zakk Wylde is known more for his heavy rock guitar, but he also brings in things like banjo rolls, which comes from his country influence;

That brings me to my next point…

Guitarists have Different Influences

All of the greatest guitarists have different influences. Angus Young from ACDC is heavily influenced by Chuck Berry. Now if you know of ACDC, read and watch Chuck Berry; the two might not look similar but the more you examine the two, you can see the direct link. For example, the duck walk/goose step that Angus Young is famous for was done initially by Chuck Berry.

In terms of playing, Chuck Berry pioneered a style of double stop licks that Angus uses strongly in most of his material.

Jimi Hendrix was influenced by a mix of styles also. His showmanship came from playing with Little Richard and he learned the idea of playing behind his head from T-Bone Walker.

Randy Rhoads, who played with Ozzy Osbourne, was known more for his heavy rock guitaring but was very influenced by classical music; just listen to Dee from the *Blizzard of Oz* album.

What are your different influences?

Styles Are a Mix of That Which Has Come Before

Styles are a mix of different styles before them anyway. For example, many punk fans might not like the Blues, but if you delve into the music, you can see that the Sex Pistols used a lot of Blues and R&B licks. Early Ramones material was surf songs sped up.

If you listen to Deep Purple you can really hear Ritchie Blackmore's classical influence and the Vivaldi style licks that he used to get that fast pedal note sound.

Ritchie Blackmore played violin before he played the guitar and he brought these licks into his playing. Many musicians were too worried about image and wouldn't have wanted to combine classical music with heavy rock but Ritchie didn't worry about stigmas. He played what came naturally from that which he had learned. And if you listen to any shredding today, you can hear a strong influence from classical music.

Sometimes influences are hardly noticeable, but once you know they're there, they become obvious. Listen to *Hotel California*. What style of music do you think this is influenced by? It's reggae because the song was released at the same time as the big reggae boom; around a similar time to Eric Clapton playing his reggae version of *Knocking on Heavens Door* or The Clash combining punk and reggae.

THE ONLY WAY TO NOT BE INFLUENCED IS TO BE FREE OF YOUR SENSES

Below is a list of songs that sound like, or have similar sounding parts to other songs that have come before them. There are of course lots more. See if you can find your own.

No one is totally original. From the moment that we are born we learn from others. It is not the end of the world if one of your songs sounds like another artists song.

Remember when you first started? Just learning a Major chord was an acheivement, and the knowledge of how to do that had to come from somewhere else.

In saying that, being 'original' or sounding unique is still something that I encourage.

SONG	BAND	T.I.S*	SOUNDS LIKE	BAND	T.I.S
Why Don't You Get A Job	Offspring	Whole Song	Obladi Oblada	The Beatles	Whole Song
Look At What You've Done	Jet	Similar Feel	Imagine	John Lennon	Similar Feel
Are You Gonna Be My Girl	Jet	intro	Lust For Life	Iggy Pop	intro
Big Bang Baby	Stone Temple Pilots	Chorus	Jumpin Jack Flash	Rolling Stones	
Smells Like Teen Spirit	Nirvana	Intro riff	More Than A Feeling	Boston	Chorus riff
I Don't Like The Drugs	Marilyn Manson	intro	Fame	David Bowie	Intro
Take Me Out	Franz Ferdinand	1:04	Trampled Underfoot	Led Zeppelin	Intro/ Verses
Fade To black	Metallica	3:53	A National Acrobat	Black Sabbath	Intro

SONG	BAND	T.I.S *	SOUNDS LIKE	BAND	T.I.S
Gives You Hell	All American Rejects	Chorus Riff	Pour Some Sugar On Me	Def Leppard	Chorus Riff
For Whom the Bell Tolls	Metallica	1:17	Fairies Wear Boots	Black Sabbath	5:42
21 Guns	Green Day	Chorus	All The Young Dudes	David Bowie	Chorus

* Approximate T.I.S = Time in song (minutes : seconds)

Exercise 7.1 Differentiate between 'Like' and 'Appreciate'

Imagine eating the best food that you have ever tasted in your life and just knowing that if your friend tried it, they would like it too. Then you tried to show your friend but your friend said "No, I only eat sausages. Not noodles, not vegetables, not anything… just sausages!"

Think about how much your friend would be missing out on. Well that is exactly what happens in the music listening world. People often get trapped into liking music based on it's appearance as they identify with that tribe.

It's the classic scenario of heavy metal kids disliking rappers, or Goths being thought of as weird by pop lovers. It may seem a bit of a generalization but it happens so much, and a lot of it is to do with appearance rather than music.

Being open to new ideas is a catalyst for growth, and 'appreciating' things that you may not necessarily 'like' is a great first step in growing musically. Continuous learning has opened me up to appreciate so many styles of music that I might have otherwise passed over without giving them a fair shot.

1. Read about and understand the word 'appreciate'. List 3 musical acts that you don't necessarily like, but appreciate.

   a. _____

   b. _____

   c. _____

What have they done that is worth appreciating?

_____

_____

_____

_____

_____

_____

_____

_____

_____

_____

Exercise 7.2 Learn Different Styles

Exploring various styles of guitar playing introduces you to many more techniques, skills and ideas than just trying one.

Great players have formed their styles through mashing up different influences.

Zakk Wylde is primarily a rock/heavy metal guitarist but shows his Southern American influences by incorporating 'banjo rolls' into his playing.

Rodrigo Y Gabriela use their heavy metal influence to add interest to their percussive style which is also formed from their Spanish background.

Contemporary guitarist Randy Rhoads played guitar for Ozzy Osbourne though tracks such as *Dee* show that he was an accomplished Classical guitarist.

1. Find 3 styles of guitar playing that you have not learned yet but may like to try in the future.

   a. _____

   b. _____

   c. _____

Exercise 7.3 Trace The Lineage!

Chapter 7 of *Use Your Buzz To Play The Guitar* is all about expanding your awareness of different players and styles and opening your mind to new influences, in order to help you grow as a musician. These exercises can all be re-visited at different points in your playing journey no matter what level you are at. Tracing musical lineage is interesting and can give you a new appreciation for artists that were in the past, in the same way that studying classic sports players can help ones game. Study Slash, and you will soon find out how much he was influenced by Joe Perry. Listen deeper to the playing of Angus Young and you can hear those Chuch Berry licks (and see him copy his famous 'duck walk')

1. Re-read Chapter One of *Use Your Buzz To Play The Guitar*. Do not skip this step, you have read it before but read it again. Repetition can help you pick up on things that you did not pick up on previously, and can help to spark off new ideas.

2. Use the four guitarists from the list you wrote down in Exercises 1.2 and 1.3 and find out who their main influences were. List multiple artists for each guitarist.

3. Record what you find in the Guitarist/Influences table on the following page.

4. After you have done all of the above in detail, read about the artists in the 'influenced by' column of your table.

FIND YOUR FAVOURITE GUITARISTS INFLUENCES

GUITARIST	INFLUENCED BY

Exercise 7.4 Sounds Like....

In our quest to be original we can often discard ideas that are good if they remind us of other artists. This is not the thing to do. Many of our favorite artists have used ideas taken from other artists, and have parts of songs that sound like other musicians' songs.

If anything, let similarities pay homage to your influences and don't be too proud to acknowledge those artists that inspired you.

1. Look over the table of songs that have parts similar to other songs, listed in Chapter 7 of *Use Your Buzz To Play The Guitar*.

2. Find your own examples of songs you like that sound as though they have been influenced from other specific songs. Use the 'Songs Sound Like Other songs' table on the following page to record your observations.

Note: Doing the exercises above can be especially useful for generating ideas for original composition and songwriting. It is also very liberating musically to stop being so concerned with whether you sound like another artist or not.

Just write music how you want to write music!

SONGS THAT SOUND LIKE OTHER SONGS

SONG	ARTIST	T.I.S	SOUNDS LIKE...	ARTIST	T.I.S

T.I.S = TIME IN SONG (Approx minutes : seconds)

How This Chapter will Help You

Following the philosophy in this chapter will help you to broaden your knowledge of music in turn **helping you to become a much more capable guitar player.**

Chapter 8 – Questions:
Ask and Ye Shall Recieve

Strings FAQ

What is the gauge of a string? Strings come in different thicknesses. With a set of 8's, the strings are light and very easy to bend, but they are also more sensitive to being bent out of tune; and some would say have a thinner sound. That may be a matter of personal preference.

If the packets high E string is .008, it means it is .008 of an inch thick. Usually people would call a packet of strings starting with this gauge 8. I recommend starting with 10's and later try both 9's and 11's to get a feel for the difference.

I put heavier strings on my strat style guitar and it pulled the bridge forward. Is there a way to fix this? Fit another spring, undo the back plate and you'll see the tremolo block. Attach another spring to the block or stretch it over the spring holder. Again I recommend looking up any of these terms that you do not understand and using online videos to help you.

Does the thickness of the string affect the way it sounds? Definitely. Thicker string = beefier tone.

What is the guitar's action? Action is the distance that the finger has to push the string downwards until it meets the fret. High action is harder to play and is usually louder on an acoustic. Low action is easier to play but more care is needed. If you lower the strings too much, it will create fret buzz.

General FAQ

What can I do to stop my fingers hurting from when I press on the strings?
The answer to that is practice more. Simple.

Is it best to play sitting down or standing up?
Most people learn to play sitting down and progress to performing standing up, unless they like to perform sitting down as well. Its usually best to learn a song while sitting down and then practice performing it standing up with a strap.

At what height should I wear the strap?
Its entirely up to you. Joey Ramone and Fieldy from Korn have it practically around their knees. George Harrison from the Beatles and Tom Morello from Rage have it pretty much around their neck. You can really wear it anywhere between. I recommend starting with it around waist height or where its comfortable.

Why do some people wrap the lead around the strap?
Looping your lead over the strap button has two very useful advantages: (1) It keeps the lead out of the way and (2) It helps to avoid embarrassing silences when standing on the lead and accidentally pulling the cable out of the guitar.

What is an active guitar?

Any guitar that includes circuitry that must be powered by a battery is active.

What is the difference between tremolo and vibrato?

Tremolo is the rapid raising and lowering of volume. Vibrato is the rapid raising and lowering of pitch. Confusion comes because what is often referred to as the tremolo arm on the guitar actually produces a vibrato effect.

What does the sus stand for in sus4 or sus2 chord?

Sus stands for *suspended*. Basic major triads are made up of the first, third, and fifth notes of a major scale put together. For minor chords you take the first, third and fifth, but you flatten the third. When you change the third and bring it back to the second, becoming a 1, 2, and 5; that is a sus2. When it is 1, 4, and 5, that is a sus4.

Do expensive guitars sound better than cheap ones?

Not necessarily. Give an expensive guitar to a guitarist who isn't very talented and he won't know how to set the tone on the guitar or the amp. Give a cheap guitar to a great guitarist and chances are he'll get it to sound pretty appealing.

The bottom line is that, although generally getting more expensive gear does give you the possibility of getting the sound a bit better, you must learn how to get the sound that you want first by learning about tone and developing your playing.

Can I use a guitar amp for my bass guitar?

You could but I would not recommend it. Once you start

getting serious about practicing with friends or home recording, you'll definitely need the enhanced tone that a bass amp can give you. You could also blow the amp speakers or both by using a bass guitar through a guitar amp.

How is a guitar tuned to concert pitch?
Concert pitch means that the note of A has a frequency of 440 Hz. The guitar strings are tuned to the notes E, A, D, G, B, and E, from low to high. A is the fifth string or the second of the thickest strings depending on how you look at it, and it tuned to A above middle C on the piano.

What is feedback and how is it created?
Feedback is when the guitar screeches at high volume. Microphonic feedback is usually due to cheaper pick ups and occurs where higher levels of distortion are used.

Harmonic feedback is when the amp is so loud that it drives the string creating a ringing singing note. This can actually sound pretty cool if you control it. An early example of this was the beginning of *Wild Thing* by the Troggs. You can also hear it in many, many songs. Check out *Radio Friendly Unit Shifter* by Nirvana.

Hardware FAQ

What is the difference between a single coil pickup and a humbucker?
A humbucker is basically two single coil pickups placed side by side. One pickup cancels the hum from the other.

Which is better - a single coil or humbucking pickups?
For warmth and volume - humbucking, for attack and percussion - single coil.

What gear do I need to sound like my favourite guitarist?
No gear will do this. Players have developed their own style of playing including subtle techniques which they have developed after years of hard work and practice. Learn to play like them first and look into the effects and equipment later.

What does a guitar's trust rod do?
Steel strings of a guitar exert up to 200 lbs of pressure on the neck and bridge. Truss rods are used to exert tension through the neck of a guitar and keep it straight.

Where is the nut on the guitar?
The nut is at the top of the fretboard before the first fret. The purpose of the nut is to stop the string at a precise point. This is called an *open string*. The nut can be made of metal, bone, plastic or a hard wood.

What are strap locks?
Strap locks are piece of gear to hold the strap firmly in place. They're especially good for energetic bands.

Important Questions to Ask Yourself

Hopefully. you will find that you're comfortable asking people questions when you want to know something. It's a major part of learning. If you don't ask your guitar teacher questions start doing so now.

Sometimes people say they cant think of any questions. You can. If you don't have any questions, it probably means that you're not moving forward enough because you are not trying to learn as much. Keep asking and keep learning.

Some good questions to ask yourself are: **"Where am I now? Where do I want to be and how am I going to get there?"** Those three questions can change the lives of business people, corporate company owners, street sweepers, athletes. In other words: *everyone*. If you ask these questions and listen to the answers and most importantly, act on the answers. You can achieve your dreams.

A Bit Each Day

When I was younger, I entered a competition in New Zealand called The Rock Quest. Rock Quest is a Battle of the Bands competition. As part of winning our regional finals to get to the next stage, we had to write down what we did each day to get the band ahead. I feel very fortunate that I had to learned to do this as it has come in handy many times since then.

I suggest getting yourself a small diary and trying at least five things a day. Even five small things will help get your music career going.

Three more good questions are:

- **What have I done in the last month to get closer to my goals?**

- **What have I done in the last week?**

- **What have I done in the last day?**

Chapter 9 – Tips:
Take Note to Speed up Your Progress!

Playing Tips

If it doesn't sound perfect slow it down until it does. One of the biggest problems with players trying to learn anything is that they try it too fast. Even if your goal is to become the quickest guitarist in the world, you will actually get there a lot faster by starting slow and getting it sounding good first. If you rush something that you're trying to learn, you'll make more mistakes and that's what's frustrating.

Think of it this way: no matter how hard a riff is, you could slow it down to the point where it would play one note and then it would have maybe a five second break and then it would hit the next note of the lick. If you can slow something down that much, it would almost be impossible to hit the wrong note. If it was ten seconds between each note, that would give you plenty of time.

Think about it like that. Every riff, no matter how hard, has the possibility of being played slow enough so that it would be hard to make a mistake. You want to play it slow like that first so that you get the riff correct. Speed will come naturally with repetition. But get the riff first; get it sounding good and then focus on speed.

If you use a pick, I recommend holding the pick with the first finger and thumb only. This allows the other fingers to be used for other things. You can use hybrid picking which is when you use the pick and the fingers together. If you hold the pick with the thumb and two fingers it can limit what you can do with the remaining fingers.

Using a metronome is a great way to improve speed, not to mention timing. There are many benefits and I won't get into them all here, but one of the benefits of using a metronome is also the fact that when you record in studios many engineers like you to use a click track, which is really a metronome that clicks on the beat that you listen to when you record.

One of the purposes for this is that, if you record your part and then another person in your band records their part seperately; the parts may be out of time when you put them together. Record to the same metronome speed, and when you put the parts together they will be in time with each other.

I recommend using a metronome before you ever even get into a studio, so when the time does come to record an album you're used to using one. You don't have to use metronomes to record an album, but I definitely recommend getting used to playing along to a metronome.

Set the metronome speed at say 60 beats per minute and then go up to 66 the next day, 74 the day after that. You will get faster quicker that way than just trying it at blinding speed straight away.

Play along to radio or shuffled songs to train your ear and help improvisation. Playing along to your favorite music is a fun way to improve on your instrument. It also helps because you are playing to something and feeling the rhythm.

Rhythm is such an important part of playing well. Rhythm also plays a big part in the feel of the music. You might get a person who's into rap but he or she might not like heavy metal. A lot of the time, its because of the rhythm. Think of it. Rap music has a different rhythm or a different feel to rock. The same goes for Waltz music. When you hear that 3, 4, even if I just play the block strings on the guitar and play at a 3, 4 rhythm, you can almost hear that waltz style straight away.

If I play blocked 16th notes and accent the first beat, it sounds like Funk. Playing along to your favorite tracks means that not only are you going to put your techniques to use, you're also going to improve your rhythm as well.

Translate pieces of music from other instruments. Translating and transposing pieces of music from other instruments is a good idea for a few reasons: (1) It helps to develop your notation and sight reading skills, (2) Different instruments have different ways of being played. Some of the different phrasings of the motifs, say from saxophone or piano, might sound different from the things you usually play on a guitar.

Practice pieces that are a challenge to improve your playing. Whenever you learn anything, you always have to set a little bit of a challenge for yourself, and hopefully if you have a coach or teacher, that person will set challenges for you too. Working your way through a challenge means that you will improve what you are trying to work on. There's no point in just doing easy songs and not having any challenge because that's not going to improve what your skills are like.

After you improve through these challenges, picking up the songs that you like will be much easier.

Tips for Writing a Solo – answer these questions:

- Do you want it to flow the song on or do you want it to stand out?
- Think about the section after the solo. What are the chords underneath the solo if any?
- What type of song is it? For example, is it a catchy hook filled songs or is it an abstract sounding psychedelic song?
- Does it need to change key, tempo, time signature, or change from major to minor etc?
- Remember, the more options you have the more chance of gold. Then you can erase the bad stuff.

General Tips

- Shortcuts make it harder in the long run. Practice slow at first, speed will come.
- One good note is better than a thousand bad ones.

- Patience pays so does perseverance.
- Don't be afraid of what you don't know.
- Be confident.
- History creates future.
- Have fun.

Tips for Improvisation

- If you stumble across a lick that you like take a mental snap shot of it and use it again.
- Repetition threads things together.
- Use an idea or theme.
- It doesn't have to be complicated to be good.
- People's ears like simple things.
- Express how you feel through the notes.

Things That Help you Want to Play the Guitar

Make Sure that your Guitar is Tuned.
Just like a rugby ball needs to be pumped up before you play, a guitar should be well tuned. An out of tune guitar will not sound good even if you play well and will not put you in the mood for practicing. Always tune up first just like the professionals.

Have Your Guitar on a Stand not Packed Away
When things are accessible, they're more likely to be used. Have your guitar out so it's easy to just pick up and play.

Listen to Music That Inspires You
People learn through imitation. Learn from the musicians that

you admire. I also find that songs with great lyrics are good for inspiration.

Don't Be Afraid To Listen To Different Music

People judge music with their eyes too much because generally they like to identify with a certain look or style. Don't be afraid to venture outside of the obvious to gain new ideas. There is more music in the world than the same old stuff that gets played over and over again on TV. Use the Internet or magazines to find out about music that you have not heard.

Set Goals

There is no magic point when suddenly you feel like you win the lottery with your playing. People get enjoyment from working towards things and achieving them. Set simple goals and when you achieve them, you will feel good in the process. It is *all* a process!

Find Out What Works

People are different. What works for you might not work for your best friend. Find out what works for you and take note of it.

Make it a Habit

People are generally good at what they do the most. When things are a habit, they are less of a chore. If you get used to practicing often, it is not that hard. Don't make things harder on yourself by being slack with practice.

Jam With Other Musicians

You will learn a lot more from other people if you are open to learning. You can learn from more inexperienced players as well as those more advanced than you. Jamming with other musicians will give you more ideas and lead to more opportunities.

Band Tips

- Have a point to each gig
- Open up for bigger bands
- Get good band shots done - make sure they have a point of difference
- Band Logo
- Write lyrics down - proof you have songs
- Good demo's, no straight burns

Important Band Info

- Keep bio to one page
- Don't bullet point it
- No blind bio's
- Make sure you have your name, contact details, and website address
- Keep written down what you'd do each day to get the band ahead
- Quality – or lack of – in related artwork can add or detract from first impressions
- Make sure you know your target audience - what age group is the majority of your audience, and what is the gender ratio?
- Write down your short-term goals, and how you plan to achieve them
- Get three good band shots done

- Make sure physical materials are labeled in a professional manner, not scribbled in vivid
- Keep everything together and well represented; it does make a difference to people who see band materials all of the time
- Don't sign any contracts without understanding them fully.

Things That Will Help Your Band

- Band harmony
- Good marketing
- You are never to good for help
- Flag or banner with the bands name
- A good name
- Play with good bands
- Work towards good night at the right bars
- Don't fight with the sound guy

When Attending Lessons

Your lessons are places for learning. Learning includes making mistakes. Never be afraid to make a mistake. Often we learn important things from mistakes. Apply this way of thinking to your guitar playing, whether it is in front of people or just playing by yourself on your own.

Watch the previously mentioned Jimi Hendrix - Voodoo Child live at Woodstock and any of Jimmy Page's solo's from Led Zeppelin at Madison Square Garden, and you will see what I mean by 'losing inhibitions'.

Tips For Guitar and Life

If you truly know what something is, you should be able to explain it clearly to another person. Be confident without being arrogant. Be humble while maintaining your self-esteem. It is one thing to want something but another thing to do it. Instead of thinking, "I should be doing," physically move yourself to action and do it. To know what something is, is good, to understand it is better. When you understand and apply your knowledge in a practical sense, that is when you will get the most out of life.

Tips for Making Contacts

Making contacts is an essential part of playing music professionally. When I was younger, I thought making contacts was kind of a sell-out thing to do. But that logic is irrational. You have things to offer the world, and the world has things to offer you. It is important that you take the opportunities that come your way. **The best way to make contacts is to surround yourself physically in your ambitions.** It is one thing to think a lot about what you want to do, but it is another thing entirely to do it.

1. Go to lots of gigs. The more gigs you go to, the greater chance you have of meeting like-minded musicians.

2. Place advertisements. People aren't gong to know about you if you don't get your name out there. It doesn't matter how good a player you are in your house; if you want to be heard, you need to make noise.

3. Make a contact book. As you make more contacts in the industry, it is a good idea to make a book with the list of people who can help you, and what they can do. It can be hard to know where to start, so I've compiled a list of the types of contacts that you should be in touch with. Bars - get to know the managers; photographers - for promotional shots; artists - for album artwork; radio gig guides - to list your shows; internet and magazine gig guides; local businesses - for sponsorship or ad placement; newspapers; other musicians - for recording and/or live gigs; music or instrument shops; studio engineers - to help with recordings.

Easy Songwriting Ideas for Bands

- Start at higher position for first verse and then at the second verse go to the lower. Use this as an idea but experiment with different variations of position change.
- Start with a one string riff, and then change to power chords when the band comes in.
- Using one string for a riff leaves room for the vocal line. This isn't a necessity, but a good technique to use occasionally.
- Incorporate D string power chords to play, either as the main riff, or for the second guitar player.

Every Week

Every week you should research the artists you are playing or listening to. Researching interesting facts about a song can be beneficial. Get songs sounding good with the audio.

When Learning New Techniques

Any time you learn a new technique or chord, try and write something with it. This will help you to get the technique good, but also encourage creativity. Look up artists of the songs in your folder. The more you know about musicians, the better a musician you will become. Learn to play different styles. The more styles that you know, the more techniques and knowledge you have to draw from when creating music. You can learn from anyone, even those that are less experienced than yourself. Don't put guitarists down if they aren't as good as you. Everyone starts at the same place. You had to and so did they.

Tips For Being a Good Front Person, Not Just a Singer

- Execute with confidence
- Don't hesitate
- Interact with the audience
- Be well rehearsed
- Eye contact with the band
- Energy
- Don't fake it
- Research other performers
- Clear vocals
- Don't put the mic past the monitors
- Don't rush
- Make the set list flow

Playing In Time Is More Important Than Playing Fast

Tips For Students

For students at school, apply the following to your school work. For older students, I think these are good ideas to remember and live by:

1. If you can try and keep organised, things won't seem to pile up so much and you won't feel under as much pressure.

2. Being lazy adds pressure because you only have to try and catch up in the long run.

3. Ask questions and if you don't understand the answer, ask again or ask someone else.

4. If what you're learning in class isn't your style, try and learn from it anyway. This can help you to avoid feeling that your time has been wasted. It can also provide you with ideas that you can use in your own music if you keep an open mind.

5. Your time at school should benefit you. Being sarcastic to those who are trying to teach you is not going to help you learn, and it will waste your time. Just because you're teacher is stupid, doesn't mean that your time should be wasted. You deserve to have your time at school serve you well. But remember it is not just up to your teacher.

Tips for Busking (street performance)

- Be confident
- Let people know what you are busking for
- Put a few coins in a case or hat to start off
- Play what you know well
- If you want a break from songs, improvise
- Busk where foot traffic is high
- Acknowledge people that give you money
- Get permission from shop owner
- Have a pen and paper with you

Organisations That Can Help You

I know what it's like to feel as if you are alone on your journey to being a successful musician, and no-one is helping you, but there are actually a lot of organizations who offer free advice and seminars. Remember, there is no point in complaining about the lack of help if you aren't getting off your butt and looking for it. Attend the seminars, sign up for the newsletters. It takes two seconds, do it.

The following are organizations in my original home country of New Zealand, which I have found helpful, but similar groups can be found around the world. Just take out the words New Zealand and put your country in:

The Music Managers Forum International
Music Managers Forum New Zealand
www.mmf.co.nz

Independent Music New Zealand
www.indies.co.nz

Guitar Association of New Zealand

APRA - The Australasian Performing Rights Association

Rock Radio
The Axe Attack

Street Posters
www.0800phantom.co.nz

Media Coach
Louise Pagonis

Music Management Mentoring
Lorraine Barry Music Management

Life Coaches

Personal growth has been such a big part of me turning my life
around and has even led to the creation of this book!
Although I have created personal growth material for you, such
as the *Musicians Confidence Course*, I strongly recommend
studying what the following self-development teachers have
written. Their brilliant teachings are also available as
audiobooks and online videos:

Jim Rohn
Jack Canfield
Bob Proctor
Napoleon Hill
Anthony Robbins

Their work will help to keep you motivated as you strengthen your mind and character. Each author and speaker has a different style, so it is likely that you will connect with some and disregard others. Just find the speaker that you connect with first, and read/listen to their advice repeatedly to keep conditioned as life's challenges will come along.

Chapter 10 - Get Out There and Do it Now! Nothing Happens If You Don't Start

My Early Experience In Bands

When I was beginning to learn the guitar, I thought I had to reach a certain level before I tried to get a band together. This is a limiting way of thinking and I encourage you to start straight away, if being in a band is eventually what you want to do. Even if you don't think you are ready, try anyway because by jumping in and doing it, you will end up in a band a lot sooner than if you wait for the right time. There is no right time. You will learn from experience.

Before I started my first band, I was in pretend bands that mimed because we were kids and couldn't play, but really wanted to. But when I look back, I realize that this was the first stepping stone. The next stepping stone was acting it out. We were getting together with friends and using our imagination. When you start you won't sound professional. Even professionals often need a few practice with each other when they're jamming for the first time together to sound any good. The main thing is that you stop procrastinating.

If you are young, and don't know what the word 'procrastination' means, I think you should look that up. If you are old and have forgotten what that means, then it's time to remember and stop doing it.

"I have missed more than 9000 shots in my career. I have lost almost 300 games. 26 times I have been trusted to take the game winning shot and missed. I have failed over and over and over again in my life, and that is why I succeed." Michael Jordan.

Where Musicians in Different Demographics Can Play

You can save yourself a lot of wasted energy by knowing where to play. Always remember that venues won't come looking for you. You have to approach them. If you are in your senior years, there are a lot of weekend warrior type clubs similar to social teams with football, that get together to jam and do gigs. Pack up your excuses. If you are under ten years old, you can start by playing in front of your class at school, and then after that, step up to the next level and try playing at the school assembly.

Free Gigs and Practice Rooms

If you really want to practice with your band, or on your own, you will find a way to do it. It's just that simple. If you don't, then you're not trying hard enough. If you can't practice at home, then you can use earphones or rent a practice room. If the cost of a practice room is $60 for three hours, the money is well spent because:

1. You will be paying for the space, so you are more likely to make use of the time.
2. There are less distractions than at home.
3. If you're in a band of four people, for example, it works out to only $15 each.

When you first start out, you may even want to make your first few shows free, just to get the experience. More people will attend, which may lead to more opportunities, and you're probably earning zero dollars from your music at that point anyway so you won't exactly be losing money. It is important from a professional point of view however, to charge or at least have some kind of income stream. Many professional artists have '**multiple streams of income**'.
Multiple Streams of Income is a topic of which I encourage you to study.

One tip: have a purpose to the gig. E.g. announcing your new bass player, or debuting a new song. It creates more interest around the show. You could also use the shows to get people to visit your website if you have one.

Open Mic's School Bands Etc

A great way to test the waters with new material or line-ups is open mics. An open mic is a show where you put your name down to play, and anyone who has put their name down can get up and play one or two songs. That means that you don't have to have a whole set worth of material, and chances are that some of the other performers will be trying out new things too. It's a great place to meet other musicians,and get used to being in front of an audience without having the pressure of a full show.

In Conclusion
Listen to your Dream, it's *Your Baby*

I have made every mistake imaginable when it comes to performing and being in bands. I have kept quiet and didn't speak up because the other guys I was jamming with were older. I have slipped on stage on dry ice. I have started a song with the lead unplugged. I have played a whole song with the lead unplugged. I have organized shows poorly and played to an empty room. I have dropped my pick on stage. When I started, I didn't have a distortion pedal because I couldn't afford one. I was a terrible singer and had much to learn on the guitar. I could go on at length, but the point is I got out and did it. You might be able to play as well as Van Halen, but if you are tucked away in your room and never get out and play, you are missing out on most of the fun.

A while back, I boarded a plane from New Zealand headed for the U.SA. to follow my dream.

At the time I was in debt, living by myself with lots of broken dreams and reminders of what 'could have been.' People thought that it was silly of me to head across the globe when I had no money and didn't know where I was going to stay.

As I gazed outside the plane window, tens of thousands of feet in the air with nothing but clouds and ocean below me, I couldn't help but smile. I had never felt so 'on track' before. With headphones in my ears the lyrics to the song I was listening to at the time seemed to fit perfectly:

Give me a ticket for an aeroplane
I ain't got time to take no fast train
Oh, the lonely days are gone
I'm comin' home

My baby she wrote me a letter

I don't care how much money I got to spend
I'm gonna find my way back home again
Oh the lonely days are gone
I'm coming home

Oh my baby she wrote me a letter

Listen to your dream and use your buzz to play the guitar
– Ryan Kershaw

Glossary

Note: These are basic explanations to make it easy for readers to understand. For more detailed descriptions, I recommend doing some research on the internet of the term you are focusing on

Accent: Emphasizing a note by playing it harder/louder than the rest

Amp: the amplifier and speaker system that you play an electric guitar through

Arpeggio: The notes of a chord played one at a time

Bend: pushing the string up or down with your finger on your fretting hand

Chord: a combination of 3 or more notes

Fret: the areas along the strings where you press your fingers

Hammer-on: the technique used where you play two notes, one after the other, but only pick the first. The second is played by striking down the finger of your fretting hand like a hammer, without picking.

Hook: A signature part of the song that catches the listeners' ear. Quite often a catchy guitar riff

Interval: The musical distance between two notes e.g A to E = **5th**

Jam: Making stuff up over music, or playing music with other people for fun

Lick: A small musical phrase played with single notes

Metronome: A device that produces constant beeps, ticks or clicks at a set speed, used to help a player develop the ability to play in time with a songs beat. The speed of the clicks is determined by 'beats per minute'.

Octave: The distance from a musical note to the next note of the same name. Also use the describe the shape played by a guitarist when playing two notes an octave apart at the same time

Palm mute: Dulling the sound of the notes slightly by placing the palm of your picking hand on or around the bridge area

Polychord: 2 or more separate chords played at the same time

Pull-off: Basically a hammer on in reverse

Riff: a short repeated phrase of music that often makes up the main tune of the guitar line

Semitone: The distance of one fret to the other directly next to it

Shredding: Playing really fast improvisation or solos

Slide: Playing a note, and then sliding along the string while keeping the pressure down with your finger

Solo: Generally a part in the song where the singing stops and the song focuses on a tune played by the guitarist

String raking: an arpeggio using blocked strings, usually played quickly on the way to a full sounding note or chord

Strum: to play across all or a section the guitars strings, with one movement

Sus: A chord where the 3rd note of the scale is lowered to the 2nd or raised to the 4th. Quite often guitarists will play a sus chord without realizing it by adding a finger or taking a finger off a chord

Tone: The distance of two frets e.g: fret 3 to fret 5 is one *tone*

Tremolo picking: rapid picking of a note, using up and down (alternate) picking

Would you like further help from Ryan Kershaw?

Ryan being presented with the Mentoring Success award by mentor and music manager Lorraine Barry (Dave Dobbyn, Bic Runga)

Guitar legend Tommy Emmanuel and Ryan Kershaw

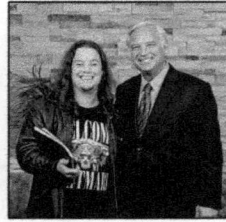

Ryan with America's number 1 success coach and author of the chicken soup for the soul series (500,000,000 books sold), Jack Canfield

Ryan Kershaw is an internationally successful musician and music teacher. He has enjoyed pushing for a closer connection between educational institutions and the music industry, and coaches clients from all around the world on achieving their goals. He is a former board member of Independent Music New Zealand, recipient of the MMF Mentoring Success award and writer for Audioculture, Muzic.net.nz and the Guitar Association of New Zealand

For further help with your music, invest in your own skills by purchasing the audiobook of Use Your Buzz to Play The Guitar, or a Use Your Buzz online course – which are available to keep for a lifetime!

For more information visit
www.ryan-kershaw.com now!